Fill My Cup, Lord

Meditations
on Word Pictures
in the
New Testament

Fill My Cup, Lord

Mildred & Luverne Tengbom

AUGSBURG Publishing House • Minneapolis

CONTENTS

The prayers on pages 34, 38, 56, 60, 72, 75, 77, 81, 123, 142, and 145, and the blessings on pages 60, 72, 76, and 141 were written by our young friend, Jean Blomquist-Shields.

AS YOU USE
THIS BOOK

The devotional part of any day or meeting rightfully should set the stage for what follows. The spirit with which we meet frustrations, the objectivity with which we face problems, the attitude we hold toward others—all can be influenced greatly by the devotional time. Hence, the devotional time is one of the most important segments of the day or meeting.

The purpose of devotional time is to quicken our awareness of the presence of God with us and to increase our understanding of what our God is like. We need not ask God to be with us. He is. But we do need to become quiet before him and realize his presence with us.

What is our God like? Some of the aspects of his character that speak most clearly to our felt needs are his accessibility, his love, his wisdom, and his power. We have tried to bear this in mind as we have selected topics for these devotionals.

If you are using these devotions to lead a group, may we make a few suggestions.

Prepare well. Do not regard this book as a convenient excuse for not having to spend time preparing. Rather, accept the book as a tool to assist you as you prepare. Plan ahead so you don't waste people's time by searching for a Bible or asking who can play the piano. Anything that gives the impression of last-minute preparation distracts.

Try to create the proper atmosphere. Gather in the sanctuary or at a simple worship center. Play peaceful music and ask people to cease talking and prepare their hearts. Any effort to slow people's pace, to draw their thoughts away from the cares of the day and direct them to God, will be helpful.

Prepare your heart, too. If possible, find a few minutes to be alone with God before you come to the meeting. With tight schedules this may be difficult, but it will be worth the extra effort.

A certain church became known for its worship services. People loved to come and worship and left with glowing faces. What was at least one of the secrets? The pastor believed in the absolute necessity of preparing himself, so when he entered the sanctuary, he carried in with him a sense of the presence of God that others quickly recognized. On Sunday mornings he arose early and went to church to pray and imbibe once again the message he hoped to bring that day. During the break between the two services, in order not to fracture the mood of worship, he explained to his parishioners that he would once again be in private prayer, but he would be happy to converse with them at the close of the second service.

If you are called on to lead a group into awareness of the presence of God, choose your devotional material several days in advance. Read it over several times. Look up the Bible passages referred to. Meditate on them. Let the message "grab" you. Only as it touches you first will it mean anything to others.

Practice reading aloud so you can read with ease, without stumbling, and with expression. Your reading of the meditation will be smoother if you omit the scriptural references given in parenthesis, but before you read the Bible reading be sure to tell the group what verses they're listening to. Practice reading the prayers, also, until you can do so effectively.

Find out what the time limit is and stay within it. If possible, allow several minutes for free prayer when you remember special needs of those in the group: illness or divorce of a loved one, sons or daughters facing critical examinations, job loss in the family. Know the peculiar difficulties involved in the occupations of the members of your group and pray for them.

Remember that you never need feel apologetic for taking time to lead the group in devotions. You are not asking a favor of the group. Rather it is on this act of worship that the harmonious working together of your group will largely depend. It may even be that through this time set apart, some will, for the first time in their lives, consciously come face to face with Jesus Christ.

Fill My Cup, Lord, the title we have chosen, is the prayer we hope will be in your heart and on your lips at the beginning of each devotional. For that, after all, is one of the foremost purposes of the devotional time.

GREEK DOESN'T HAVE TO BE "ALL GREEK" TO YOU

Do you have parents or friends for whom English is a second language? Have you seen them shake their heads and mutter, "There's no way to say it in English"?

All languages have limitations. Some languages are richer than others. And that is why, when we try to put into words a concept which we have conceived and understood in another language, we run into problems. Even God faced this problem when he had to try to convey to humans heavenly and spiritual concepts. Earthly languages, in many cases, were too impoverished to adequately express celestial truths.

The Hebrew and Greek languages are rich in imagery, rich in words that have multiple meanings, and rich in the selection of words available to express one idea. In many instances our English language is not as rich, which limits our understanding of some of the important concepts of the Bible.

The purpose of this devotional book is to examine the meanings of certain Greek words. As we come to understand the pictures behind these words, new rays of light will shine on even familiar passages of Scripture. We shall discover that certain words, such

13

as "fellowship," mean something quite different from what some of us have thought.

There were basically two types of Greek in use at the time the New Testament was written: classical or literary Greek and nonliterary or koine Greek. Classical Greek was the language used by the scholars and philosophers of the day, the "book language." Koine Greek was the spoken language, and in a number of cases it had been influenced by other languages.

The Greek New Testament is considered one of the best sources of the nonliterary koine Greek of that day. In addition, scholars refer to Greek papyri, ostraca, and inscriptions. Papyri are documents written on sheets of ancient paper, for the most part Egyptian. Ostraca are documents written on pieces of broken pottery, and inscriptions are usually inscribed on stone.

Under the category of documents fall personal documents, business documents, legal documents, official documents, family letters, love letters, tax receipts, bills of sale, marriage contracts, business contracts, records of lawsuits and court procedures. In all, at least 50,000 documents have been published.

The bits of pottery are fewer as these were the tablets of the poor. Most are records of accounts and tax receipts.

The inscriptions on stone are dominated by sepulchral and official inscriptions.

In addition, the writing of Epictetus, a Greek Stoic philosopher born in A.D. 60, teaches us much about Greek of that day. This is also true of the apocryphal books, which were considered by church councils for inclusion in the Bible but for various reasons were not admitted. Works of pagan authors also have been studied.

14

The Greek Old Testament has proven to be a valuable source, too. There are many Greek translations of the Old Testament. The best known is called the Septuagint, named thus because tradition said 70 scholars worked on it.

From these various sources scholars have learned more and more about the Greek language and the meanings behind the words.

The Greek language has been a "living" language, that is, a spoken language, for more than 3000 years. Like all other languages it has gone through many changes. Without the help of scholars we could not properly understand many of the terms used in the New Testament.

As we delve more deeply into the fuller meaning of Greek words, our understanding of the text grows also. We hope this little book will bring you added understanding of God's Word, and with it inspiration.

philia (fee-LEE-ah)   love
philein (fee-LANE)   to love

LOVING WITH PHILIA LOVE

Let us pray.

L ord, when we look upon our own lives, it seems Thou hast led us so carefully, so tenderly, Thou canst have attended to no one else. But when we see how wonderfully Thou hast led the world and art leading it, we are amazed that Thou hast time to attend to such as we. We praise and thank Thee. Amen.   —Augustine

Our Bible reading is from John 16:27 and 1 Corinthians 16:22.

The meditation

Philia (fee-LEE-ah), the noun, and *philein* (fee-LANE), the verb, are beautiful Greek words. They recall an atmosphere of a crackling wood fire on a winter's evening with the snow falling softly outside. Of catching a whiff of home-baked bread. The sense of security that comes with crawling into bed with papa and mama while thunder shakes and rattles the windows and lightning bathes the room in startling white light. Of being greeted by a warm hug and a kiss and pot roast in the oven when you come home at the end of the day.

Philia is being rocked in the rocking chair when

your dog has died and later arms around you when a dearly loved family member has died. It is the tender concern your husband shows for you when you are pregnant. *Philia* is hearing your wife say, "I love you," before you drift off to sleep at night. It is your friends giving a surprise birthday party for you, or hearing your parents on the other end of the line when you're away at college, calling just because they want to hear your voice. *Philia* is bringing mother breakfast in bed on Mother's Day, even if the kitchen is a sticky mess. *Philia* is all this and more.

Philia means to regard affectionately, even to kiss, to love, and to cherish. It is the special love we feel toward those who are closest to us, our spouse, parents, children, sweetheart, and dearest friends. *Philia* is spontaneous emotion from an overflowing, grateful, responsive heart. And, wonder of wonders, *philia* and *philein* are used to describe God's love for his Son, Jesus' love for his friends, God's love for *us,* and *our* love for God.

In this day of store-bought bread, fast-food meals, tired, tense, anxious husbands and wives, baby-sitters, day-care centers, sauna and dance studios, lavish allowances and gift cars, and professionals even in soul care—when people are consumed with loneliness and starved for love—how meaningful to learn that God cherishes this kind of love, *philia* love, toward us.

Let us look at some of the references where the word for "love" is *philia* or *philein*.

John 5:20 declares: "The Father [God] loves the Son [Christ]." In John 11, when Jesus' relationship to Lazarus is described, it is said: "Jesus wept. So the Jews said, 'See how he loved him!'" In John 20:2 John is described as "the one whom Jesus loved." And in Jesus' farewell talk to his disciples we find these astonishing words: "For the Father himself loves you, because you have loved me and have believed that I came from the Father" (John 16:27). Equally astonishing are Paul's words in his first letter to the Corinthians when he declares that if any one does not love the Lord with *philia* love, that is, with warm, affectionate, caring, cherishing, feeling, family love, that one should be accursed (1 Cor. 16:22).

What a different aspect this gives to our relationship to Jesus. A formal, intellectual faith will not suffice. Our Lord loves us tenderly, affectionately. He puts his arms around us, smoothens our hair, rubs our backs, and kisses our tears away. In return he longs for this kind of heart-stirred, misty-eyed, feeling love from us.

One of the unique things about our Christian faith is that we meet and find God in one another. I can better understand God's *philia* love for me when you love me with *philia* love. And as we love one another with *philia* love, we both experience God's love for us, but also, in an almost sacramental way, we express our *philia* love for God. Thus Paul urges: "Love one another with brotherly affection" (Rom. 12:10), using the word *philostorgos* (fee-loss-TOR-goss), a combination of *philia* and *storge,* the Greek word meaning specifically "family affection or devotion." The Christian community, God and all God's children, is not a society, but a *family*—a family reflecting the beauty of our God as we experience and give *philia* love to our Father and to one another.

So let us love our God and one another with *philia* love: warm, cherishing, feeling, affectionate, demonstrative love.

19

Let us pray.

Our Father, we stand overwhelmed at the way in which you love us. Our hungry hearts long and thirst for your *philia* love. Gratefully we receive it. We sit before you with open hearts. Pour in your love. Fill our cups, O Lord, fill them up. Fill them to overflowing so love will spill over to those around us. Through us reach out and touch others with your matchless love. In Christ's name. Amen.

Receive God's blessing.

"The grace of the Lord Jesus be with you. My love be with you all in Christ Jesus. Amen" (1 Cor. 16:23-24).

WHEN PHILIA LOVE RUNS OUT, TRY AGAPE

Let us pray.

O Lord, give us more love, more self-denial, more likeness to Thee. Make us kindly in thought, gentle in word, generous in deed. Teach us that it is better to give than to receive, to forget ourselves than to put ourselves forward, to minister than to be ministered unto. Amen.

—Dean Henry Alford

Our Bible reading is from Psalm 103:8-17.

The meditation

Philia is a warm, choice word. Why then was it used only rarely in New Testament writings while another word for love, *agape* (the noun), was used almost 120 times and *agapan* (the verb), more than 130 times? Simply because *philia* has limitations. God's love knows no limitations, so a new word had to be found to describe God's love.

Philia is limited in outreach. It is spontaneous love for those we love dearly, a love that we don't have to "work up" or produce. We just *do* love our family. Sometimes we also "fall in love." But we are commanded to love also our neighbor and our enemy.

21

Philia love doesn't spring into being naturally toward enemies. Nor is it easy to experience *philia* to any significant degree for those of different cultures who do not know Christ, but we are admonished to love them too. In all of these instances and more, *philia* falls short.

Philia is limited also in its durability. *Philia* is fine for demonstrative affection and tender feelings when we are in a convention with like-minded people. But *philia* might not be enough to carry us through cleaning someone's house when illness strikes or repairing plumbing for an elderly person or taking a divorced woman's children on a day's outing so they can enjoy male companionship.

Philia may suffice to love our parents or children when all goes well. But *philia* may run dry when month after month and year after year we have to care for a stroke-injured, senile parent. *Philia* may even die when a wayward child repeatedly scorns and wounds parents and brings dishonor to the family name.

And even if we should succeed in cultivating close friendship with a neighbor, *philia* surely falls short in producing the right kind of loving feelings toward that neighbor when her radio awakens us at five every morning or her son zooms deafeningly up and down our street on his motorcycle. Because of the limitations of *philia,* a new word had to be found to describe God's limitless love.

Agape is the word for that type of love. Loving with *agape* means willing other people's highest good, no matter who they are, what they are like, or what they have done. *Agape* is steadfast, unwavering, unchanging love.

Friends of mine, who had married very young, were riding rough waters in their marriage. *Philia* love was running out. Through counseling sessions they began to grasp the necessity of loving with *agape* love. They learned not to think in terms of a life span—a frightening length of time, especially when you don't know if you want to live with that person any longer at all. They determined instead to try to practice *agape* love a day at a time. An amazing change took place. Harmony, peace, contentment, and joy began to fill their home.

But in the learning process one always encounters minor failures, slipping back into old ways. So it happened one day for Linda. She and Chris had planned to build an arbor for hanging plants outside their bedroom patio door. Linda awakened feeling crabby. Humid summer temperatures climbed more quickly than usual. By midmorning the heat was torrid. The day screeched along with fussy, whining children getting in the way. The arbor stubbornly refused to come together right as the two amateurs hammered away. Frustrated, Linda reverted to old habits and began to rail at Chris. Rail, rail, rail— all day. At five she went in to throw something together for a meal. Opened the frig. Slammed it shut. Opened the cupboard. Shut it with a bang. Wheels squealed as she backed her little car out of the driveway. Twenty minutes later, lugging two heavy brown bags, she headed for the kitchen only to be greeted by shrill, angry children's voices from the bedroom and Chris' electric drill whining in the garage.

"Do you have to run that thing?" she shrieked at Chris as she tore down the hall to silence the children. When she came back, Chris was quietly sweeping up the shavings. A new wooden plaque sat in the kitchen window. Long and narrow, it said, "I think I love you." Linda stared and then dissolved in a flood of tears on Chris' shoulder.

The day had been too much for *philia* love. It was time for *agape* to take over. Understandably, Chris was experiencing a conflict, as we all do before we begin to love with *agape* love, for *agape* love means deliberately choosing to seek the other's highest happiness no matter how much we *feel* like hating them or spanking them or dumping them at that moment.

Agape love. God's love for us. Steadfast. Unchanging. Unending. Self-giving. Durable. Trustworthy. If God so loves us, we ought also to love one another —with *agape* love.

Let us pray.

I stand all amazed, Jesus, at the love that you offer me. I marvel at the grace that you proffer me so freely. I weep that for me you were crucified, that for me, a sinner, you gave your life and died. I think of your suffering to rescue me. Such love and such pity—how can I forget? So, Jesus, I bow and adore you. I worship and praise you. I give you my heart and my will, my self, my being, to love and to live for you. Amen.

Receive God's blessing.

May your covenant God, who is in your midst, heal your faithlessness, love you freely, renew your love, rejoice over you with gladness, and exult over you with loud singing. And may nothing ever separate you from God's love made known through Jesus Christ. Amen.

THE COSTLY COVERING

Let us pray.

O God, so many thoughts and concerns clutter our minds. Silence the restless clamoring so we may hear you speak. Amen.

Our Bible reading is from Hebrews 9:1-5 and 11-12.

The meditation

I had never known how much her husband's long black robe meant to Minna until that day I talked with her in her kitchen.

"I thought it was a good idea when the congregation voted that their pastor be robed for Sunday worship services," I began, "but I didn't think you would be so enthusiastic about it, Minna."

Minna was kneading bread. The fragrant aroma of molasses, anise, caraway seed, and yeast rose from her bowl.

"You thought I was too plain for anything fancy like robes?" Minna asked, punching the dough and turning it over. "Well, but you don't understand. That long black robe is such a good *covering*. Ole's suit is getting so old it won't stay in press." With the back of her arm she brushed away a stray whisp of brown hair from her eyes. "That robe covers

25

everything. Only six inches of pants stick out at the bottom." Her blue eyes twinkled. "I don't have to worry any longer about Ole's pants splitting when he's standing up front with his back to the congregation. He's all safely covered now."

Since the beginning of time, people have longed for a safe covering. It's a giant step back in time from Minna's cozy country parsonage of the early 1950s to the Garden of Eden, but let's take it.

After our first parents fell into sin, they immediately felt the need for a covering. God gave them leather suits to take the place of the fragile grass skirts they had put together. We can see symbolism in the leather, for that covering called for the shedding of blood.

The next cover of significance referred to in the Bible is the lid or cover of the ark of the covenant. The ark was a cabinet in which were placed three items: the tablets of the law, which were God's guiding words for his people; Aaron's rod, depicting God's power; and a bowl of manna, representing God's provision. We read in Exodus 25:17 (LB): "And make a lid of pure gold, $3\frac{3}{4}$ feet long and $2\frac{1}{4}$ feet wide. This is the place of mercy for your sins." Alternate translations for "place of mercy" would be "mercy seat" or "place of making propitiation."

The ark resided in the tabernacle, in the holy of holies. Only once a year did the high priest enter this place and approach the ark to commune with God, and then only after he had offered blood sacrifices—first for his own sins, then for the sins of his people—and then sprinkled blood on the cover of the ark.

Integral parts of the golden cover for the ark were two cherubim. Artists, trying to reconstruct what these cherubim probably looked like, have sketched the figures of animate beings with the heads of hu-

26

mans, to represent their intelligence; the front quarters of oxen, to depict strength; the hindquarters of lions, to depict courage; and the wings of eagles, to suggest free flight. The cherubim faced each other, with wings touching. From the space over which the wings hovered, it was said, God spoke to his people.

Cherubim are first mentioned as being placed by God at the entrance of the garden to keep out Adam and Eve after they had sinned. Some scholars believe that this earliest reference to cherubim was in reality a reference to a storm cloud that hovered at the edge of the garden. In Psalm 18 God is described as coming down from heaven with thick darkness under his feet. "He rode on a cherub," we read, "and flew; he came swiftly upon the wings of the wind. He made darkness his covering around him, his canopy thick clouds dark with water" (vv. 9-11).

In the Bible clouds symbolize the presence of God. The cherubim—or cloud—in Eden portrayed two things. A chasm had separated God from his people; God had become inaccessible. At the same time, in love God was present, preventing his people from eating the tree of life and living forever, which in their sinful state would have been disastrous.

Whether the cherubim mentioned in Genesis actually were storm clouds, we do not know. But we do know that biblical writers later began to represent them as animate beings, and considered them an order of angels.

When the cherubim were placed on the lid of the ark, they symbolized the inaccessibility of God to his people because his people had sinned. At the same time, the ark itself represented the presence of God. So we have an interesting paradox: the ark representing the presence of God, and the cherubim on the lid saying: "Stay at a distance."

27

But if we think about it, we can understand it. Within the ark were the tables of the law, Aaron's rod, and manna. Remembering what they represented, we understand that God has never utterly forsaken his people. He continues to be present with them in the law he has given to instruct, in his power manifested many ways, and in his daily provision for all. At the same time, sin, that terrible intruder, brought about a break of fellowship between God and his people. And this fellowship could be restored only by the shedding of blood. Only as the blood of the sacrifices was poured on the lid of the ark did the lid become a mercy seat or place of mercy.

The blood of the goats and lambs of the Old Testament was but a symbol of the sacrifice that God's Son, Jesus Christ, was called upon to make. Only because of Christ's sacrifice has God again become accessible. But the way is now open. We may boldly approach him directly at any time. And this is the meaning of "expiation," as we find it referred to in 1 John 2:2: Jesus Christ "is the expiation for our sins, and not for ours only but also for the sins of the whole world."

The Greek word for expiation is *hilasmos* (hih-loss-MOSS), and one of its meanings is "covering." Christ became the blood covering for our sins so we might approach God without fear or guilt.

We must never lose sight of or minimize the awfulness of what happened when Adam and Eve sinned. The gap of separation was real and so deep and wide that only God himself, in Christ, could bridge it. We have a covering for our sin now, but that covering has been purchased for us at an incomprehensible cost to God, and we must never forget it.

Let us pray.

Lord, make more real to us the price you paid, that we might be able to approach you again without fear and guilt. May that realization motivate us to live as we should. Amen.

Receive God's blessing.

May the one who suffered for you sanctify you through his blood. Amen.

WIPED OUT

Let us pray.

Make us, O God, sorry for our sins and grateful for your forgiveness. Help us to love as you love. Amen.

Our Bible reading is from Colossians 2:13 and 14.

The meditation

Jacob Mugisha, a 36-year-old who escaped to Kenya from Idi Amin's military regime in Uganda, tells how in Uganda he was forced to kill more than 20 fellow prisoners, one a close friend. He was ordered to hit the back of their necks as hard as he could with a heavy iron bar and then pound their faces to a pulp so they could not be recognized.

"I'll never be able, in all my life, to forget what I have done," he lamented. "I wish somehow I could wipe it from my memory."

We can understand that those memories will haunt. Jacob Mughisha is not alone. All of us have memories that make us wince. Times when unkind, harsh words escaped from our lips, words that cut deeply and broke, not necks, but spirits. Or times when we treated someone wrongly, lied or cheated, gossiped or tread over other people in our hurry to get to the top. Times when envy and resentment burned in our breasts. We've erred so often that sometimes we feel as though we are traveling through life collecting citation after citation. We know too that the Bible tells us a day of reckoning will come when we shall face our Judge, and he will hold all these citations in his hands. We feel uneasy as we think about this. In fact, we don't want to think about it at all.

The apostle Paul used a slightly different figure of speech than "citation." He spoke of us going ever deeper into debt. In his day many people were so poor that, just to stay alive, they were forced to borrow from a rich person. When the rich person extended the loan, he would write on a piece of papyrus paper or vellum the name of the creditor and the amount of the debt, and the creditor would sign it.

Occasionally it happened that a wealthy man would forgive a creditor. The benefactor would take the piece of papyrus or vellum, and he would acknowledge settlement of the debt in one of three ways. He might draw a line through the statement of indebtedness, or with a nail he might drive the piece of papyrus or vellum onto the door of the creditor, or he might post it on the town bulletin board. This act would declare publicly that this man's debt had been paid. His credit was good. Occasionally all three procedures were followed.

But because papyrus and vellum were scarce and expensive, one more thing was often done. After the notice had been posted for all to see, the benefactor would rip out the nail, and remove the papyrus or vellum from the board. The ink contained no acid, so it did not penetrate the product on which it was inscribed. With a wet cloth the benefactor would wipe clean the papyrus. No trace of the poor man's account would remain, and in this way the benefactor could use the vellum again. These recycled manuscripts even had a special name: palimpsests.

It is this figure which Paul uses. Our sins have made us debtors, he declares. The account is entered against us. In fact, so great has become our indebtedness that we stare at it with a feeling of hopelessness and despair. We have no way to ever repay it.

At this point the Son of God steps in. In one stupendous, sweeping act he gathered together all the sins of the entire world and bore them in his body on the cross. Christ was lifted down from the cross, limp and lifeless, because settlement for our sins demanded his very life, but the parchment listing our sins—now crossed out—remained nailed to the cross for all to see. Paul tells the Colossians: "And you, who were dead in trespasses . . . God made alive together with him, having forgiven us all our trespasses, having canceled the bond which stood against us with its legal demands; this he set aside, nailing it to the cross" (Col. 2:13-14).

The word for "having canceled the bond," *exaleiphein* (ex-ah-LAY-fain), means also to "wipe off and wipe away." Having announced to the world that our debt has been paid, God wipes the papyrus clean.

Corrie ten Boom describes it this way: "God takes our sins and throws them into the depths of the sea. Then he puts up a sign that says, 'No Fishing!' "

Because of Christ's death, God simply does not see my sins any more. They have disappeared. He has wiped them away. When we face our Judge, the citations in his hand will be blank.

How staggering this thought is! How impossible

to take in! How undeserving we feel! But God declares this is so, and God cannot lie.

Thus I may enter each new day knowing God is holding none of the sins and failures of yesterday against me. I may close each day and go to sleep serenely, his forgiven, washed-clean child. My concern now is to remember at what fearful cost to God my past record was obliterated and to live motivated and controlled by grateful love for him.

Let us pray.

O God, my Savior, I accept your forgiveness. I forgive all who have injured me in any way. I thank you that I can walk in newness of life. Amen.

Receive God's blessing.

May the God of love who has washed, sanctified, and justified you in the Lord Jesus Christ be with your spirit. Amen.

agoradzo (ah-go-ROD-zoe)
to buy in the market
exagoradzo (ex-ah-go-ROD-zoe)
to buy out of the market
lutroo (loo-TRO-oh)　to set free

NOT BORN FREE, BUT SET FREE

Let us pray.

O God, time seems to go so quickly, and there is always so much to do. We ask now that you would help us forget our busyness for these moments, that we may come to you fully and completely. Amen.

Our Bible reading is from Galatians 5:1.

The meditation

The large square cement blocks in the courtyard of the Anglican cathedral in Zanzibar, East Africa, threw back at us the searing heat of the tropical sun.

"We are standing on the site of the old slave-trading block," our guide said. "The slave trade decimated the population of Africa by 100 million. For every slave who reached a foreign shore alive, 26 died on the way."

"One hundred *million?*" I whispered to Luverne. He nodded, his usually cheerful face somber.

34

I sat down on a rock under one of the huge trees. What tales those cement blocks could tell us, I thought. What shrieks, wails, and sobs had pierced the air here. How many teardrops of anger and frustration had wet those blocks! What savage, primitive, animallike anger had broken loose! How many cowed men and women, with broken, bleeding bodies, had crouched, waiting their turn to be hauled up on the auctioneer's platform, for him to point out their bulging muscles, shapely legs, or sound teeth. What shame! What fear! What hopelessness! What despair!

"Come inside the church," our guide said, leading the way into the cool shadows of the nave. My eyes squinted momentarily, then focused, following the long aisle to where it ended in a flight of marble steps that led to an altar.

"The altar," said our guide, "was built over the site of the whipping post."

I shut my eyes. The thought of human beings, rearing and roaring, flailing and fighting, and everything blurred for them by blood and sweat and tears, was too much. Surely, I thought, few places in the world have concentrated in one small area as much anguished suffering as this slave market of old. Who of us can begin to comprehend what it must have been like? Alex Haley, in his book *Roots,* has given us insight into the horror of it, but it still seems unreal and unbelievable.

For Paul the slavery picture was vivid. The Greeks of Paul's day brought home prisoners of war to sell on the slave market. Because Paul was so familiar with this horrible practice, he used it frequently as an illustration to describe our bondage to sin.

In Genesis 4:7 sin is described as outside of people, crouching at the door. But not for long. The temptations were so alluring and promised so much that the door of the human heart swung open. Sin entered. "Sin dwells within me," Paul laments.

"This sin," Michael Quoist cries, "possesses me as the spiderweb holds captive the gnat. It sticks to me. It flows in my veins. It fills my heart. I can't get rid of it. I run from it the way one tries to lose a stray dog, but it catches up with me and bounds joyfully against my legs."

Having possessed us, sin robs us of our freedom. "I am carnal, sold under sin," Paul agonizes. Nor is Paul alone. "All are under the power of sin," he goes on to assert. The picture is of a child, a minor, who is under the control of a parent or guardian, or an army under the control of its commander.

The picture worsens. The more we sin, the more helpless we become to stop sinning. We become "captive to the law of sin which dwells in [our] members" (Rom. 7:23).

We are like the prisoner-of-war, who is cramped and crippled, confined to a cage too low to allow him to stand and too short to permit him to stretch out and lie down. But even for the shackled and starving prisoner, a little glimmer of hope lingers. "When the war ends," he consoles himself, "we'll be sent home. Our desperate situation cannot continue for ever."

But if we think sin will loosen its grasp on us and let us go, we are mistaken! Our captor will not release us, even if the war ends. Rather he will inform us that we are his slaves. Paul uses this figure of speech in Romans 6:17 and 20, and Jesus used it in John 8:34: "Truly, truly, I say to you, every one who commits sin is a slave to sin."

Bit by bit we realize that our freedom is gone

completely. We can try and try to do only good, but we cannot. In fact, the harder we try, the more we seem to fail. Slowly it begins to penetrate our dull minds that this slavery will be for life, that our children will be born into it and continue in it all their days.

However, let us suppose our master decides to put us up for sale, even as sometimes happened to Greek prisoners-of-war. Mingled emotions churn within us, but despair and fear predominate, plunging us into deepest darkness. Never have we felt so utterly helpless.

At that moment a commanding figure strides into the slave market. When the bidding begins, he calls out the highest figure and throws down the silver required to purchase us. Then, picking up the chain that imprisons us, he leads us out of the marketplace.

Once outside the city our new master motions us to sit down under a tree. In the cool shade he reaches over and unfastens the chain that has bound our wrists and ankles. Then he reaches in his bag, draws out a writing pad and a pen, and busies himself writing. When he is finished, he hands us a document. We stare in disbelief. The parchment is a letter of manumission, a statement that the master who has bought us has also set us free.

"Stand up," he says. "You are free. Go your way, and God go with you."

The Greek words that describe the acts of the closing scene of our little drama are *agoradzo* (ah-go-ROD-zoe), which means to come into the marketplace to make a purchase; *exagoradzo* (ex-ah-go-ROD-zoe), which means, having made the purchase, to take it out of the marketplace; and *lutroo* (loo-TRO-oh), which means to issue the papers of emancipation. *Lutroo* frequently is translated "redeem."

We do well to remember that all illustrations break down when we try to see meaning in every detail. So too with this one. We *have* been bought with a price—but the price paid was not silver, but Christ's blood. Also, the price was not paid to Satan. But, in some mysterious way that defies the finite understanding of most of us, the spilling of Christ's blood has set us free from the power and consequences of sin. Because of Christ's death, the grave and the Evil One do not hold us captive any longer.

How do we find this freedom? When we realize we are slaves to sin, we cry out with Paul: "Who will free me from my slavery?"

That cry signals our release. We feel the chains drop. We hear the liberating words of our new Master as he proclaims to us the forgiveness of all our sins. With joy we cry out: "Thank God! It has been done by Jesus Christ our Lord. He has set me free" (Rom. 7:25 LB).

We can testify to this experience, and tens of thousands join us in this testimony. Is it yours also?

Let us pray.

Our Savior, release us from the shackles of sin. We are weighed down and burdened. Remove these chains, that we may truly experience the freedom you alone can give. Amen.

Receive God's blessing.

May the grace of our Lord Jesus Christ, who has set you free from the bondage of sin, be with your spirit. Amen.

DO YOU RETURN YOUR CALLS?

Let us pray.

Lord Jesus, give us ears that are quick to hear your call and hearts that will respond. Amen.

Our Bible reading is from Hebrews 3:1 and 7-8; 1 John 3:1; Mark 6:7; and 2 Corinthians 5:9-10.

The meditation

Back in 1896 when Mr. and Mrs. John B. Rea of Anaheim, California, went to the door of their ranch home to call their two daughters, Kate and Ella, to supper, little did they realize the lasting impression their calling made on those who heard. At that time Anaheim was just a small town that had sprung up to serve the many owners of orange groves scattered around the countryside. But with the great push westward, industry soon intruded. As bulldozers uprooted the groves to make way for buildings, the town of Anaheim gave promise of becoming a city. So as city planners laid out and named streets, the name for the street running by the Rea home seemed to be ready-made and waiting. "Kate-Ella," the neighbors said, smiling at

39

one another. Today, because our home lies only two short blocks off Katella, I often think of Kate and Ella, many years ago, running to answer their parents' call to supper.

The gospels are full of accounts when Jesus sent out his call: John! Peter! Mary! Martha! Matthew! It was an invitation to follow him.

And he continues to call today. "I have called you by name," he declares in Isaiah 43:1: "You are mine." Many of us know what it has been like to hear that call.

So the Greek word *kalein* (kah-LANE), which we translate "call," carries, first of all, the meaning of an invitation issued. It is up to us whether we accept that invitation or not.

Katella Avenue was named after the girls who were called and responded, but in the Christian walk, those who respond to the call are named after the one who calls. Those who hear and respond to God's invitation, his call, are then given a name by God. They are called his children. Many know what it is to bear proudly a family name that has won esteem and high regard. How amazing that we are permitted to bear Christ's name! John never ceased marveling at this. "See how very much our heavenly Father loves us, for he allows us to be *called* his children—think of it!" he exclaims (1 John 3:1 LB).

So *kalein* also carries the meaning of being "named," of being called by a name.

Being a child in a family involves not only privileges, but responsibilities as well. Work is shared.

The call to duty is repeated often in the New Testament. Paul said he had been *called* to be an apostle. That meant work. In his parable of the man going on a journey, Jesus said the man *called* his servants, that is, he summoned them to take care of his business for him while he was gone. Many of us who hear Christ's initial call and who are delighted to be called his children are wearing earphones and listening to other tunes when Christ's call or summons to duty comes.

But *kalein* has yet another meaning.

I once inadvertently made a U-turn where a U-turn was not allowed. Later I was called or summoned to court to answer the charges against me.

So too, even as a time of reckoning comes for the child who has not washed the car or wiped the dishes or done the chore he or she has been called to do, a time of reckoning, a summoning, a calling will come for the child of God. We shall be summoned before the judgment seat of God to give an account of what we have done with what God has entrusted us to use. We'll wish then we hadn't worn those earphones, won't we?

The progression of thought is easily seen.

God *calls* me, he invites me. I respond. God then *calls*, that is, he names me. He calls me his child. Because I am now his child, he *calls* me again, this time to share in the work that needs to be done in his home. And finally, at the end of my life, he will *call*, or summon me to report on how I lived the life he entrusted to me.

Kalein. Call. God's call to me. How do I respond?

Let us pray.

Jesus calls us; o'er the tumult
  Of our life's wild, restless sea,
Day by day his clear voice sounding,
  Saying, "Christian, follow me."

Jesus calls us! In your mercy,
  Savior, make us hear your call,

Give our hearts to your obedience,
Serve and love you best of all.

—Cecil Frances Alexander

Receive God's blessing.

"To those who are called, beloved in God the Father and kept for Jesus Christ: May mercy, peace, and love be multiplied to you" (Jude 1-2). Amen.

thalpō (THAL-poe)
to soften, keep warm
to cherish, comfort

CONTACT COMFORT

Let us pray.

Speak to us, Lord, during these few quiet moments as we focus our thoughts on you. Amen.

Our Bible reading is from Psalm 42:1-2.

The meditation

Magnus Landstad, one of the great Norwegian hymn writers, grew up in Osksness, a village among the frozen fjords of the Norse seacoast. In later years Landstad wrote: "The waves of the icy Arctic sang my cradle lullaby; but the bosom of a loving mother warmed my body and soul."

Christ loves his people with a warm, comforting, protective love. Paul refers to this in Ephesians 5:29, where he says that Christ nourishes and cherishes the church.

The Greek word for "cherish" is *thalpō* (THAL-poe). *Thalpō* means literally "to heat, to soften by heat or to keep warm." The picture is that of a mother hen gathering her little chicks under her wings.

"Hide me in the shadow of thy wings," the psalm-

43

ist prayed (Ps. 17:8). In singing of the love of God, the psalmist exclaims: "How precious, O God, is your steadfast love! We find protection under the shadow of your wings" (Ps. 36:7 TEV). And in yet another psalm he exclaims: "Oh to be safe under the shelter of thy wings!" (Ps. 61:4). The psalmist was feeling a need for warmth, for being held and protected, for being loved and cherished.

Psychologists are discovering the relationship between the physical feeling of warmth and the feeling of being loved. Some psychologists put a motherless monkey in a cage with two surrogate mothers, one a wire mesh "mother," and the other a terrycloth "mother." The wire-mesh mother "held" a bottle from which the monkey drank. But as soon as the monkey finished his bottle, he ran back to the terrycloth mother to seek warmth and comfort. And when a number of motherless baby monkeys were allowed to be together in the same cage, they huddled close together, sucking their thumbs and putting their arms around each other, seeking contact comfort and warmth.

Gone are the days when mothers are encouraged to prop up bottles for their babies in their cribs. Instead, parents are urged to hold and cuddle their children while they feed them. Children need to feel the closeness and warmth of their parents' bodies.

During our time in Africa, when our children began to smile with the winsome grin of toothless six-year-olds, we had to send them 300 miles away to boarding school. They would be gone for three months, then come home for one month, return to school for three months, home for a month, etc. Midterm we would visit them for a weekend at school. During those weekends the four used to compete as to who would sit next to us, and our laps were seldom empty.

"I don't know why it is," our eight-year-old said to us once as she snuggled down, "but little kids just want to be near their mothers and dads."

Even we adults know the strength and peace we draw from the embrace of those who love us. This is the kind of loving we promise to give when we take the marriage vow to love and to cherish.

Paul, in writing to the Christians at Thessalonica, declared that he loved them too in this tender way, "like a nurse taking care of her children," he wrote (1 Thess. 2:7). In writing to the Philippians he called them "my beloved," "my joy and my crown," "whom I love and long for," "whom I hold in my heart." And when the Christians at Ephesus said good-bye to Paul, they wept and embraced him and kissed him. A tender, affectionate, demonstrative, warm, touching love characterized Paul's affection for his fellow Christians.

"In love of each other be tenderly affectioned" is counsel for us too.

Christine, a woman in a membership class in one of our congregations, was asked to give a brief autobiography. She began, but soon broke down. Through tears and sobs she poured out her story, her accent telling the group she was European-born.

When her father died of cancer, she had been sent as a child to live with her grandmother. When her grandfather died, her grandmother remarried. But the step-grandfather was a cruel man, who sexually assaulted Christine, even to the point of Christine's falling unconscious.

Then World War II descended on her continent. Because German strains ran in her family's blood,

45

Christine, at 15, was sent to a hard-labor camp. Escape came when she married an American serviceman. He brought her to the United States, but a year later, after she had given birth to a child, he walked out on her.

Three years later she married another man whom she did not know well, only to discover, too late, that he was an alcoholic and a gambler. He too finally walked out on her.

Over the years she was left alone to support her son and herself. Her burden grew heavier when her teenage son turned to drugs. She was able to find help for him in time. But now she had received word that her sister had committed suicide. She felt guilty because she had always pointed out to her sister her shortcomings, but she herself had never admitted to God or anyone else that she had done anything wrong. Sobbing, she told the hushed group that she had spent one whole night weeping and confessing the bitterness, anger, and hatred she had felt toward God.

One of the members of the group got up and walked over to the lamenting woman. Gathering her in her arms, she held her close. Christine put her head on the shoulder of the other woman and sobbed out, "Sometimes the little child in me still longs to have someone hold me and love me and assure me everything will be all right."

At times like that, what can we say? But we can do what this sensitive woman did. We can, with our arms, enclose the hurting, suffering one, and let comfort and love pass from our body to the one who needs it so much. As she was held, this distressed woman experienced the acceptance of the group, and with it the forgiveness and acceptance of God. It marked a turning point for her, and the past 11 years she has been engrossed in developing a new life in Christ.

Thalpō. Contact comfort. It is one of the ways we can make real to others how God loves and cherishes them.

Let us pray.

Dear God,
Under your wings I'm safely abiding;
Tho' the night deepens and tempests are wild,
Still I can trust you; I know you will keep me;
You have redeemed me, and I am your child.

—William O. Cushing

Thank you, Father, for your love: warm, protecting, and reassuring. Amen.

Receive God's blessing.

As a mother hen shelters her chicks under her wings, so may the Lord almighty gather you to himself. As a bird hovers over its nest to protect its young, may the angels of God hover over you to protect and defend you. Amen.

HE'S GOT YOU
AND ME
IN HIS HANDS

Let us pray.

$\mathcal{D}$ear Lord, quiet our fears, increase our faith, and make steady our trust as we come to you now. Amen.

Our Bible reading is from Revelation 2:1.

The meditation

Any thoughts of lurking danger were far from Florence Anderson's mind as she walked from the bank to her car in a fashionable suburban shopping center. It was noon. The warm southern California sun felt good on her back. Birds were singing. She shifted her bag to her other hand so she could unlock her car door. A young man approached her with a smile.

"Can you tell me what time it is please?" he asked.

Florence pushed up her sleeve to look at her watch. Suddenly, she felt her glasses fly off her nose and pain seared through her fingers as her purse was snatched from her. She screamed, but by the time someone realized what had happened the young man had slipped into his car and driven away. The $100

48

bill Florence had just withdrawn from the bank was gone. She had held her bag tightly, but not tightly enough. Her assailant was too strong for her.

None of us would think of doing so, but let us say Florence had enclosed the bill completely in her fist. The thief then would not have made off with it as easily. In the first place, he might not have guessed she had a $100 bill in her hand. If he had attacked, a struggle would have ensued, and Florence would have had some time to fight back. But at the same time it might have been even more disastrous for Florence in the end, for Florence quite likely would have been more severely injured.

The word for "to hold" in Revelation 2:1 is *kratein* (kraw-TANE): "To the angel of the church in Ephesus write: 'The words of him who holds the seven stars in his right hand.'"

The word "to hold" appears in the first chapter of Revelation also, where the son of man is said to hold in his right hand seven stars, but the Greek word in this instance is *echein*, which means to grasp or to hold as you would hold a book or a bag in your hand. But *kratein*, which is used in the second chapter, means to completely enclose within one's hand. This same meaning is conveyed in John 10:27 and 28 when Jesus describes how he cares for us. He declares: "My sheep hear my voice, and I know them, and they follow me; and I give them eternal life, and they shall never perish, and no one shall snatch them out of my hand."

Thus our Lord holds us. "Thou art my hiding place," the psalmist sang (Ps. 119:114). God encloses me in his hand, and even if the enemy finds me and seeks to snatch me, my Lord will fight back at him. Injury will come to my Lord first. And I

49

need not fear, for my Lord is mightier than any assailant and can easily overcome in any skirmish.

Nor does our Lord hold only me in this way. He holds the whole church. He measures the waters of the world in the hollow of his hand—surely he has room in his hand to hold all his children. Because of this his church has survived through all the centuries, vigorous and alive even when it has been a minority group surrounded by hostility.

During World War II the German missionaries working in East Africa had to leave their areas of work. The fledgling church was left on its own. Did it die? No, it flourished and grew more than it ever had before. The Lord had his church in his hand.

Martin Luther wrote:

> It is not we who can sustain the Church, nor was it our forefathers nor will it be our descendants. It was and is and will be the One who says: "I am with you alway, even unto the end of the world." As it says in Heb. 13: "Jesus Christ, the same yesterday, and today, and forever." And in Rev. 1: "Which was, and is, and is to come." Verily He is that One, and none other is or can be.
>
> For you and I were not alive thousands of years ago, but the Church was preserved without us, and it was done by the One of whom it says, "Which was," and "Yesterday."
>
> Again, we do not do it in our lifetime, for the Church is not upheld by us. . . . Again, we can do nothing to sustain the Church when we are dead. But He will do it of whom it is said, "Who is to come," and "forever."

So do not be anxious. Our Lord has you in his hand. If *you* were grasping his hand and stumbled, ah, then you easily might drop his hand and fall. But the Lord has his hand around yours, yes, even more, he has *you*, all of you, enclosed in his strong and mighty hand.

And do not fear the future of his church either. Social changes threaten to undermine Christian principles and morals. The future looks forbidding. But the Lord God of heaven and earth has his church in his hand—and all history too!

Let us pray.

God, you are our refuge and strength. You are ever aware of our problems and fears. We have no business worrying or doubting you. You continue to reign, the all-wise, the almighty God. Your eternal plan will not be thwarted by human action. Civilizations may rise and fall. The earth itself one day will be destroyed. But you will not leave us. You are forever our certain and sure refuge and strength. Help us hear you saying, "Relax. Quit fretting. Remember who I am. I am still in control." We praise and worship you. Amen.

Receive God's blessing.

May God be with you, and may his presence free you from anxiety and fear. May he strengthen you, protect you, and enclose you in his victorious right hand. May you hear him saying to you, "Fear not, I will keep you." In the name of the Father, the Son, and the Holy Spirit. Amen.

WHEN HURT IS IMMENSE

Let us pray.

O God, our forgiving Savior God, we come to say we are sorry for all the wrong things we have done: for grumbling over our work and doing it carelessly; for hurting, disappointing, and failing people who need us; for caring so little that so many are living without knowing you; for disobeying and grieving you and often loving you only in a cool, indifferent way. Forgive us, Lord. Amen.

Our Bible reading is from Matthew 5:4.

The meditation

Penthein (pen-THAIN) is gray-haired Jacob, grasping tightly the arm of his chair with his left hand, putting up his right hand as though to shield himself, and turning his face away as Joseph's blood-drenched robe is brought to him. "It is my son's coat," he sobs. "Some wild animal has killed him. My son Joseph has been torn to pieces" (Gen. 37:33 TEV).

Penthein is Naomi, the old widow, and Orpha and Ruth, the two new widows, clinging to one another, weeping and kissing one another.

Penthein is King David putting a veil over his face

52

and crying, "O my son Absalom, my son, my son Absalom!" (2 Sam. 18:33).

Penthein is Mary, the mother of Jesus, at the cross, and Mary Magdalene outside the tomb of Jesus, weeping.

Penthein, usually translated "mourn," is an exceedingly strong word, throbbing with deep emotion. The word *klaiein* (KLY-ain), which means "to weep," often is linked with *penthein.*

Seven times *penthein* is used in the New Testament. It sometimes describes the sorrow following tragedy or bereavement, as in Revelation, where it portrays the mourning of bewildered, worldly people after their city Babylon is destroyed (Rev. 18:11, 15, 19). Jesus used the word when he asked why the friends of the bridegroom should mourn while the bridegroom was still with them (Matt. 9:15). In these instances *penthein* is used to describe the grief experienced because we have lost or anticipate losing someone or something we have prized highly.

James uses *penthein* in a different way when he talks about the remorse sinners experience when they confront a righteous but loving God and become miserably conscious of their sins. *Penthein* is the despised publican, the man in the place of power who has used his office for graft, not daring to enter the church door, but standing outside and crying, "God, be merciful to me a sinner!" *Penthein* is the apostle Paul recalling with tears, "I not only shut up many of the saints in prison . . . I punished them often. . . . I persecuted them even to foreign cities."

But to feel so sorry for our sins that we actually mourn is an experience with which most of us are not familiar. How does this happen?

Sorrow for sin cannot be commanded into existence. It springs into being in much the same way that faith grows. Have you ever noticed that when you focus on your faith, examining, evaluating, weighing, and measuring it, it seems to shrivel and shrink? Only when we shift our focus and concentrate on our matchless Savior does faith blossom and grow.

So too with godly sorrow for sin. First our love for God must grow, and will grow, as we walk with him, dwell in his Word, and understand how much he loves us. Then as we realize how much we have hurt the one who loves us the most, sorrow will creep into our hearts.

The realization of our sinfulness and unworthiness often is a long time coming. William Barclay makes an interesting observation in regard to the titles Paul gave himself as he moved on in life.

In his letter to the Galatians, which some scholars believe could have been written as early as A.D. 48, Paul refers to himself as "Paul an Apostle." He was eager to assert his coveted position of respect and authority.

Years pass. In A.D. 55, when he writes to the Corinthians, he confesses, "I am the least of the apostles, unfit to be called an apostle" (1 Cor. 15:9).

Yet another eight years pass. He writes to the Ephesians: "I am the very least of all the saints [church members]" (Eph. 3:8).

And as his life draws to a close, the aged apostle confesses humbly, "I am the foremost of sinners" (1 Tim. 1:15). The longer Paul lived, the more aware he became of his sinfulness.

Penthein is used in yet a third way. It can be our mourning when someone we love is losing the way (1 Cor. 5:2; 2 Cor. 12:21). When we are gripped with this sorrow, we become partners with our suf-

54

fering Savior. As Paul expressed it, we help to fill up and make complete his sufferings.

For *penthein* is Jesus weeping over the city of Jerusalem and crying out, "How many times I wanted to put my arms around all your people, just as a hen gathers her chicks under her wings, but you would not let me!" (Matt. 23:37 TEV).

Penthein. To mourn. An emotion so fierce that it cannot be hidden within the secret regions of our hearts, but breaks forth in weeping. The grief that follows bereavement. Godly sorrow for sin, our own and the sins of others. A mellowing, purifying experience for those who dare to draw close to the cross of Jesus Christ and take a long look.

Let us pray.

But tears of grief cannot repay
The debt of love I owe;
Here, Lord, I give myself away:
It's all that I can do. Amen.
—Isaac Watts

Receive God's blessing.

Now may our Lord Jesus Christ himself, and God our Father, who loved us and gave us eternal comfort and good hope through grace, comfort your hearts and establish them in every good work and word. Amen.

HELP
WANTED

Let us pray.

We come with burdens; uplift us.
We come with failures; restore us.
We come with sorrows; uphold us.
Rejoice with us, O Lord;
We come to you with joy! Amen.

Our Bible reading is from Isaiah 61:1-3.

The meditation

Our Arab guide evidently noticed my upturned face and puzzled expression. We were standing inside one of Cairo's theaters.

"No roof," I said.

Our guide grinned. "No rain," he said. "One-tenth of an inch a year."

The next day we were together in the tower overlooking the city of Cairo. A light brown haze hung over the city.

"Smog?" I asked.

Our guide shook his head. "Dust," he said.

I followed the sweep of our guide's hand as he flung out his arm. Through the dust I was able to make out the faint outlines of the pyramids.

56

"Oh, my goodness!" I exclaimed. "I hadn't realized the pyramids were that close to the city."

Our Arab friend looked at me.

"Ma'am," he said, "the desert creeps right up to the city. Only irrigation and sprinkling keep it away. Egypt is a land of sunshine, but as one of our proverbs states: 'All sunshine makes a desert.'"

The proverb attached itself to my mind like a burr. That night in our hotel room I told Luverne about our conversation and the proverb.

"I've always puzzled over the beatitude, 'Blessed are those who mourn,'" I confessed. "I've never been able to understand how it could be said that it is fortunate to mourn. But if 'all sunshine makes a desert,' we can consider ourselves fortunate if trouble or grief comes into our lives, can't we? I don't like trouble, but I sure don't want to dry out like the desert either."

Luverne replied, "I think that when we understand the full meaning behind the word *parakalein* [pa-ra-ka-LANE], which is translated 'comforted,' we can understand better where to place the emphasis in that verse. I don't think the emphasis should be placed on 'mourn' but instead on 'you.' Blessed or fortunate or happy are *you* when *you* mourn *for*."

The Greek word *parakalein* originally meant simply "to call to one's side." But as time went on the word took on more and more meaning until it became very rich.

In the first place, *parakalein* means to have someone to call to our side who can comfort us. We all can survive terrible tragedies if we can call God himself to our side to love, support, and comfort us. God comes to us in many ways, perhaps most often

57

through his Word and through his people who help us.

Parakalein also means "to call to one's side someone who can counsel."

What widow has not felt the need of counsel? After Jim Elliot was murdered by the Auca Indians of Ecuador, his wife, Elizabeth, turned to her brother for advice. What should she do? "You are one of the few who know the language of the people among whom you live," her brother reminded her. "You must stay on and teach them God's word." That was difficult counsel to give a sister and difficult counsel to accept. But Elizabeth Elliot followed her brother's counsel, and because she and others stayed on, there are Christians there today.

Parakalein also means "to summon to one's side an advocate, a lawyer, who will plead our case for us." In this instance the mourning referred to is mourning because of sins we have committed. To those deeply burdened by guilt because of wrongs done, what comfort to know that they may call to their sides none other than Jesus Christ, the Son of God. He will plead their case, for he himself already has paid the penalty for their misdemeanors.

Parakalein has yet another meaning: to exhort, encourage, stimulate, energize, and excite.

"Where the Holy Ghost dwelleth," Martin Luther said, "he will not suffer a man to be idle, but stirreth him up to all exercises of piety and godliness, to the love of God, to the patient suffering of afflictions, to prayer, to thanksgiving, and the exercise of charity toward all men."

I remember back to my early 20s when the poverty, ignorance, sickness, and spiritual darkness which submerged the people of Nepal deeply stirred my heart. As I cried out to God, weeping and protesting, the Holy Spirit hauled me up short with: "What are you going to *do* about it?" I dried my tears, packed my bags, and went to India. For seven rewarding years I lived and worked among the Nepali people, conducting literacy classes, teaching Bible classes, doing evangelistic work, and, with my colleague, a nurse and a midwife, caring for the sick. Together we witnessed God at work bringing light into troubled minds, healing to suffering bodies, and spiritual life and hope where despair, self-centered living, legalism, or hopelessness had reigned.

Thus, in my case, the work of the Paraclete, the Holy Spirit, was two-fold in my heart and life. First he wrung my heart with the sorrow God feels for his lost children, and then he stirred me to action. The *parakalein* the Holy Spirit offered me was not sweet, sentimental sympathy because I felt so troubled about the distress of the Nepalese, but rather a swift "kick in the pants" to get me moving. Quite a difference! But in the going I *was* blessed.

So then we may say:

Blessed are *you* when you grieve following bereavement, if you are God's child, for you have God, the Holy Spirit, himself whom you may call to your side for comfort.

Blessed are *you* when you are perplexed, because you have one you may call to your side for counsel.

Blessed are *you* when you sorrow over personal sin, for you may call to your side as your advocate the Lord Jesus Christ, the Righteous One. He will plead your case because he himself has paid the penalty for your wrongs.

Blessed are *you* when you mourn over the injustices and wrongs you see done to others, for the

Holy Spirit will stir you to action and energize you to fulfill your calling.

Three aspects of suffering cause us to mourn: bereavement because of loss, sorrow for sin, and grief over injustices done to others. In three different ways God will come to our side: as the God of all comfort and wisdom, as Jesus our Advocate, and as the Holy Spirit our Energizer.

No wonder Jesus said, "Blessed are *you* when you mourn," for you have one whom you can call to your side. How different it would be if we did not have him!

Let us pray.

Our precious God, only you know the sufferings, the disappointments, the failures, and the sins which drape our lives in sackcloth. Lighten our burden with hope and the knowledge that you are the compassionate Comforter as well as the competent Advocate, ever-present, ever-faithful. Strengthen us and stir us in the face of injustice to speak boldly, think keenly, and act bravely. Amen.

Receive God's blessing.

May the compassion of our God comfort you. May the counsel of the Righteous One defend you. May the Spirit of the Holy One stir you to action. Amen.

CHRIST'S ENGAGEMENT RING FOR HIS BRIDE

Let us pray.

Jesus, thy boundless love to me,
No thought can reach,
   no tongue declare;
Unite my thankful heart to thee,
And reign without a rival there!
Thine wholly, thine alone, I am;
Be thou alone my constant flame.

—Paul Gerhardt

Our Bible reading is from 2 Corinthians 1:21 and 22.

The meditation

Modern affluent people aren't very interested in heaven. That is, not until it's *their* time to die. Then many of them discover fear surging inside. "Hold me till the fear in me subsides," a song pleads.

Dr. Kübler-Ross, the psychiatrist who has listened to the fears of hundreds of dying people, believes the predominant fear people have of dying is the fear of extinction. Even Christians may be troubled with this fear and wonder if there really is a life

61

beyond the grave. To reassure us, to allay our fears, and to give us something tangible to hang on to, God guarantees the life to come. "God has given us the Spirit as a guarantee," Paul wrote (2 Cor. 5:5).

The Greek word for guarantee is *arrabon* (air-ah-BONE). From studying the Greek documents, we understand that the word meant a pledge or earnest of any kind. It was the down payment obligating the contracting party to make further payments. For example, one document states that an entertainment troupe had been engaged to perform at a stated function. To guarantee to the troupe that they would indeed be called on to appear, a sum was paid them in advance.

Paul picks up this commercial term and uses it to illustrate God's guarantee to us of continuing life beyond the grave. Ken Taylor has interpreted 2 Corinthians 5:1-5 beautifully:

> For we know that when this tent we live in now is taken down — when we die and leave these bodies—we will have wonderful new bodies in heaven, homes that will be ours forevermore, made for us by God himself, and not by human hands. How weary we grow of our present bodies. That is why we look forward eagerly to the day when we shall have heavenly bodies which we shall put on like new clothes. For we shall not be merely spirits without bodies. These earthly bodies make us groan and sigh, but we wouldn't like to think of dying and having no bodies at all. We want to slip into our new bodies so that these dying bodies will, as it were, be swallowed up by everlasting life. This is what God has prepared for us and, as a guarantee, he has given us his Holy Spirit" (LB).

But how do we know the Holy Spirit does indeed dwell within us? The Holy Spirit makes himself real to us in countless ways. By making Jesus an alive,

62

personal reality to us. By helping us to believe and trust. By assuring us God has forgiven us. By filling our hearts with peace, love, joy, long-suffering, goodness, patience, self-control, and meekness. By giving us understanding of the Bible. By encouraging and empowering us. By giving us distinctive gifts. By guiding us.

We could go on and on. Once we begin to think about it, the indications that the Holy Spirit does indeed dwell within us are so numerous that our question marks straighten their backs and become exclamation marks of joy and amazement. The presence of the Holy Spirit with us takes the "if" out of our questions about life after death.

The Holy Spirit is also, as Paul expressed it, only "the first installment of all that [God] is going to give us" (2 Cor. 1:22 LB). What does this mean? Simply that the joy, peace, patience, goodness, long-suffering, meekness, and self-control which we see released in our lives now—and which thrill us—are but a tiny portion of what we shall experience in our hereafter life with God. How shall we be able to contain all the love and joy and peace? Truly, how heavenly it will be when all of us overflow with patience, long-suffering, and meekness! And how innumerable will be the expressions of goodness and kindness! No wonder Paul, in thinking about all this, exclaimed: "What no eye has seen, nor ear heard, nor the heart of man conceived, what God has prepared for those who love him, God has revealed to us through the Spirit" (1 Cor. 2:9).

In the Greek language of today, a derivative of *arrabon, arrabona* (are-ah-BONE-ah), is an engagement ring. We may say that the Holy Spirit is the engagement ring Christ has given us, his bride. This ring is his guarantee that a wedding will follow, and

63

a feast, a home, an inheritance, shared life and work —all of which, we are confident, will leave us completely overcome at God's goodness toward us.

Let us pray.

O God, we thank you for your promise of life beyond the grave. We thank you that you have given us the Holy Spirit to live within us and to reassure us that the things that are invisible are real, and that we can trust you. Strengthen our faith and enable us to live always with eternity's values in view. In Christ's name. Amen.

Receive God's blessing.

"Now to him who is able to keep you from falling and to present you without blemish before the presence of his glory with rejoicing, to the only God, our Savior through Jesus Christ our Lord, be glory, majesty, dominion, and authority, before all time and now and for ever. Amen" (Jude 24-25).

paidagōgos (pie-da-goe-GUS)
child-tender

A FINGER-WAGGER OR A PARENT?

Let us pray.

O God, we thank you for the Bible, written and preserved for us. Help us to treasure it enough to study it. Strengthen our faith. Fill us with the Holy Spirit. Amen.

Our Bible reading is from Romans 8:1-2.

The meditation

Who trains and disciplines children in today's world? Parents? Baby-sitters? Teachers? The long arm of the law? Influential members of the children's own peer groups? Grandparents and aunts and uncles? All of these, in varying degrees.

The Greeks of Paul's day placed good manners, courteous behavior, and meticulous personal grooming of their children so high on their value scale that whenever it was at all possible, they hired a special person to train and discipline their children. This person was called a *paidagōgos* (pie-da-go-GUS). Usually a man, he was a combination of guardian, disciplinarian, personal servant, and chaperone. He was *not*, however, a teacher.

65

The New American Standard Version of the Bible has translated *paidagōgos* as "child-conductor." Why the term "child-conductor"? The *paidagōgos* had as his special responsibility to conduct the children to school, to see that they did not dawdle or behave in an unacceptable way while in public.

The story is told of Socrates conversing with a young lad.

"But you understand, don't you," Socrates asked the young boy, "that life won't permit you to do just as you want to do?"

"Oh, yes," the boy responds, "I already have someone who lets me know every day of my life that I cannot do as I wish."

"And who is he?" Socrates asks.

"My *paidagōgos*, of course," the boy replies.

"And when does your *paidagōgos* discipline you?" Socrates asks.

"When he takes me to my teachers," the lad responds.

Some *paidagōgos* were good men, genuinely interested in and desirous of the best for the children in their charge. But sometimes parents were careless in choosing a *paidagōgos*, perhaps hiring a slave too old to do any other type of work.

Paul used the word *paidagōgos* twice. In his letter to the Corinthians he wrote: "Though you have countless guides [*paidagōgous*] in Christ, you do not have many fathers. For I became your father in Christ Jesus through the gospel" (1 Cor. 4:15).

Paul was saying, "Probably many will remind you of all the do's and don'ts and shake their fingers at you every time you break God's law. But finger-wagging, nagging, and insisting that you obey the law will never make a Christian of you. I didn't treat you that way. I presented Christ to you in such a

66

way that you wanted to turn your will over to him. And when you did that, you became a Christian, and I became your father in the faith."

When Paul used the word *paidagōgos* in his letter to the Galatians he declared the law itself a *paidagōgos*. Phillips has translated Galatians 3:24-26 this way: "The Law was like a strict governess in charge of us until we went to the school of Christ and learned to be justified by faith in him. Once we had that faith we were completely free from the governess's authority. For now that you have faith in Christ Jesus you are all sons of God."

That is, Paul said, until Christ came and you could put your trust in him, the law was useful in keeping you from going astray. It also acted like a plow preparing the ground of your heart to receive the seed of the gospel. For as the law was preached to you day after day, and as your overseers reminded you every time you broke the law, the realization of your own inability to go God's way dawned on you. You began to feel the need for a Savior. However, when you put your trust in Christ, you immediately were set free from the wagging finger of the law or enforcers of the law. You are no longer, in God's sight, a minor. You no longer need a *paidagōgos*. Now no one has the right to stand over you with a long list of rules and see that you fulfill them or discipline you if you don't. You are accountable to God. You will live life from now on, not from the stance of "I should do this" or "I must not do that," but rather with the spirit that cries out, "Teach me thy will, O Lord. I delight to do thy will."

Have you known what it is like to be whiplashed by someone who forever reminds you of the law? Have you been able to break free from that by throwing yourself on Christ to save you? Have you been set free from the law of sin and guilt and made alive in Christ Jesus?

Perhaps you yourself have been guilty of being a *paidagōgos*. Paul says that there are many of them around, but what we need are parents in the faith.

God's law is good. It needs to be preached and taught. It is useful in showing us the right way and convincing us of our need of a Savior. We must not throw out the law.

But people will be set free and churches will grow as we abandon the role of finger-wagging enforcers of the law who demand that we obey God's rules to please him. Instead, our liberated lives will draw people to Christ, and thus we shall become mothers and fathers in the faith.

Let us pray.

Help us, O God, to live and walk as liberated people of God. Amen.

Receive God's blessing.

"May the God of peace provide you with every good thing you need in order to do his will, and may he, through Jesus Christ, do in us what pleases him. And to Christ be the glory forever and ever! Amen" (Heb. 13:21 TEV).

WHEN THE WALLS COME TUMBLING DOWN

Let us pray.

Enable us to respond to your love, O Lord, so we may be fully reconciled to you. Amen.

Our Bible reading is from Romans 5:6-11.

The meditation

"Here, take this needle and stick it into my hand."

Amy Carmichael, the missionary who rescued hundreds of Indian children from lives of prostitution in Hindu temples, held out a needle to the little Indian girl standing before her.

"Why?" The little girl drew back.

"You insist on continuing to do naughty things," Amy explained. "We've tried and tried to teach you, but you just won't learn. Now I want you to stick this needle deep into my hand."

"But why?" the girl persisted.

"I don't know how else to show you that every time you steal and lie it is as though you stick a needle into my heart," Amy cried.

69

The little girl saw Amy's eyes fill with tears. The little girl's lower lip began to quiver. Thowing the needle to the floor, she flung her arms around Amy.

"I don't ever want to be naughty again," she sobbed. And that day did indeed mark a turning point for that little girl. Melted by Amy's love for her, she exchanged a rebellious, willful spirit for a humble, teachable one. She was reconciled to the missionary who had befriended and saved her.

Amy did not need to be reconciled to the little girl. She had cherished only love in her heart for her from the beginning. And no matter how naughty the little girl had been, Amy's love had not changed. It was the little girl who needed to be reconciled to Amy. And the desire to be reconciled was born in her heart when she caught a glimpse of how much her waywardness hurt Amy. Then she began to realize that Amy really loved her very much.

So, too, does God love us. As we struggle to understand with our finite minds how Christ's death on the cross "works," we may easily misunderstand the purpose of that atoning sacrifice. Christ bore our guilt, we say. Christ died to wipe out the charges against us. But this he did, not to reconcile God to us. This he did, not to appease a God who had become angry at us and who had withdrawn his love from us. Rather, Christ died to reconcile us to God.

"It is all God's work," Paul explained when he wrote his second letter to the Corinthians. "It was God who reconciled us to himself through Christ. . . . God in Christ was reconciling the world to himself" (2 Cor. 5:18-19 JB).

The Greek word for reconciliation is *katallagē* (kah-tah-lah-GAY). It is a compound form from the simple verb meaning "to change." Frequently the word was used to indicate the exchange of one thing for another. In the course of time it took on the added meaning of reconciliation, enmity being exchanged for friendship.

In Old Testament times God called the prophet Hosea to portray to his people that it was they who needed to be reconciled to their God. Hosea was to make this lesson clear to them by his treatment of his erring prostitute wife. Over and over Hosea went in search of his wife, to bring her home again. His love for her never wavered. Hosea did not need to be reconciled to Gomer. He never ceased loving her. But Gomer needed to be reconciled to Hosea, to exchange her unfaithfulness for love and faithfulness and her multiple lovers for her one true, loyal husband.

So too God has never given up on us. "How can I give you up!" he exclaims in the Book of Hosea. "How can I hand you over? . . . My heart recoils within me, my compassion grows warm and tender. . . . I am God and not man, the Holy One in your midst, and I will not come to destroy" (Hos. 11:8-9).

We can never fully fathom the meaning of the cross. But surely we can understand that on the cross Christ pulled aside the veil that hangs over the heart of God and let us glimpse a little of the anguish and hurt God experiences when we persist in going our own willful way, thinking we can live without him. The revelation of his unwavering love for us breaks down the walls we have erected between our God and us, softens our hard hearts, starts the tears flowing, and makes of us new persons. We gladly exchange independence for dependence, pride for humility, willfulness for submission, and enmity for friendship. Instead of continuing as strangers to God, we become his sons and daughters. And that is the meaning of *katallagē*, reconciliation.

71

The prodigal's father walked every day to the gate and looked down the road to see if his wandering son was on his way home. The gate stood open. The door to home stood open. The father stood with open arms.

And so does our God. He waits for us to come. Let us, therefore, be reconciled to him.

Let us pray.

Our ever-patient God, countless times we have caused you pain by our sinful ways. Awaken us so we may fully realize our sins and sincerely repent and be reconciled to you, our ever-faithful Lord and Savior. Amen.

Receive God's blessing.

May our Holy God, forgiver of all our sins, grant you the fullness of peace that comes with the wonder of reconciliation. Amen.

COLOR-COORDINATED GRACE

Let us pray.

Our Father, quiet our hearts. Give us understanding of the many ways in which we are tempted, so we will not lose out on the best you have for us. Amen.

Our Bible reading is from 1 Corinthians 10:13.

The meditation

My friend came running, rushing to get into church before the doors closed. She sighed deeply.

"What's wrong?" I asked.

"Nothing new and earthshaking, really," she said as we slipped into a back pew. "Just another of those sibling quarrels. The green-eyed monster reared his head again."

The green-eyed monster. We all are familiar with the tag given to jealousy and envy.

If we let our imaginations play freely, we could give colors to other temptations also.

Despair surely must be a deep black. The lure of success and riches undoubtedly glitters like gold. When enthusiasm for life dries up and nothing inter-

73

ests us any more, life becomes a drab gray. Anger flares red; resentments also. Cool, calculated plotting to get to the top, even at expense to others, could be colored icy blue. For every temptation a color.

Poikilos (poy-KEY-loes), the Greek word used to describe temptations, has been translated "many kinds" or "various." "Count it all joy, my brethren," James wrote, "when you meet various trials" (James 1:2).

A literal translation of *poikilos* would be "varicolored." In the Greek language of Paul's day *poikilos* was used, for example, to describe the iridescent colors of a peacock's tail.

Significantly, Peter used the same word when he wrote about the grace of God. "As each has received a gift, employ it for one another, as good stewards of God's varied grace" (1 Peter 4:10). "Each one of you has received a special grace, so, like good stewards responsible for all these different graces of God, put yourself at the service of others" (1 Peter 4:10 JB). God's grace also is varicolored.

Thus we may say for every varicolored temptation, God has color-coordinated grace to match it. The grace God gives us to withstand temptation may be as varied as the temptations are.

When Christ was tempted by the devil, he used the written Word of God to resist the devil. Three times Christ said, "It is written."

Jesus spoke to Peter of how Satan had desired to have Peter, that he might sift him as wheat. "But," Jesus said, "I have prayed for you that your faith may not fail." In this case, the varicolored grace to fit Peter's temptation was Christ's intercessory prayer on his behalf.

Paul was tempted to pride. God himself stepped into Paul's picture and gave him a "thorn in the flesh" to keep him from becoming complacent or proud. Just what that thorn was, Paul never stated, but it was a token of God's varicolored grace, to match Paul's temptation.

Often God can use us as transmitters of his varicolored grace to those who are being tested. The passage in Peter where God's grace is described as "varicolored" states that God has distributed gifts of grace to each of his children. As we use these gifts to help one another, we shall be able to help others stand in times of temptation. The particular gifts to which Peter refers in this section are love, hospitality, speaking words that seem to come from God, and the oft-ignored gift of helping. These gifts can help us succor one another during times of trial.

But the word *poikilos* also means intricate or complex. Temptations can be very complicated. "I can't see my way out," we sometimes complain. Again, we may take courage. God's grace can match the most complicated temptation. He is able to find a way out for us.

"You can trust God," Paul assures us, "not to let you be tried beyond your strength, and with any trial he will give you a way out of it and the strength to bear it" (1 Cor. 10:13 JB).

Varicolored temptations? Yes, but also varicolored grace to match them. Complicated situations? Yes, but God will reveal a plain path for us to follow.

Let us pray.

Our God, we give you thanks for your kaleidoscope of grace. Like the glorious rainbow brightening the storm-weary sky, your grace touches and heals, inspires and encourages, calms and uplifts. We thank you for *poikilos* grace to meet our *poikilos* trials and

75

temptations. Help us always to remember you are with us and will see us through our many difficult times. Amen.

Receive God's blessing.

May the Great Artist, whose palette holds the varied colors of grace, paint your life with grace to make you radiant in every temptation. Amen.

THE COMMUNITY OF HOLY SINNERS

Let us pray.

You have given us the gift of life, O God. Help us to use the miracle of our minds, souls, and bodies for you. Amen.

Our Bible reading is from 1 John 1:3.

The meditation

Dr. Robert J. Marshall, former president of the Lutheran Church in America, called Christ's earthly church "a family for each other." Mary, called to be the mother of Christ, and Joseph, called to protect and provide for the little family, shared what they had and were so they could be "for one another."

Basically, this is the thought behind *koinonia* (koy-no-NEE-ah), the Greek word we have translated "community" or "fellowship."

In classical Greek the word most often was a business term meaning "partnership." However, it also carried the meaning of "community," people bound together and unified by common interests. As the years progressed, the word took on the meaning of "generous sharing."

77

In colloquial Greek, *koinonia* was used to characterize three different relationships: partners in business, mates in marriage, and a person's relationship to God.

For Christians *koinonia* is a New Testament word. It carries three meanings: community, partnership, and generous, unselfish sharing.

The Woodbridge Congregational Church, on July 18, 1651, in formulating the covenant under which they hoped to operate as a congregation, beautifully expressed the meaning of *koinonia* in one of their articles:

> We freely and cheerfully give up ourselves, each to the other, to become one lump and one stick in the Lord's hand and will (the Lord assisting us) submit ourselves one to another in the fear of God, watch over one another, bear one another's burdens, taking the same love one of another and doing all things, becoming those of the same body and whose heart is one and way one in the Lord.

Koinonia has been made possible for us only because of Christ's *koinonia*, his sharing with us by having taken on himself our sin and guilt. In turn, Christ invites us to share with him his suffering, death, life, and kingly authority. To make visible to us his desire to do this, he left with us the water of Baptism, the cup of wine, the loaf of bread, and the printed page. As we use these we experience *koinonia*, communion with him in worship, prayer, and personal devotion.

As we are drawn into partnership with the Savior, our lives take on meaning and we spontaneously reach out to a hurting world, allowing the compassion of Christ to flow through us. We experience *koinonia* in all three of its aspects: community, partnership, and generous, unselfish sharing.

Let us consider at greater length the meaning of *koinonia* as expressed in a community or through communion.

Koinonia of community has its roots in being members of the same family, God's family. Paul writes of the impossibility for light and darkness or believers and unbelievers to have spiritual communion together (2 Cor. 6:14-18).

Communion, both between God and us and between us and others, may be developed as we converse on certain levels. The late psychologist from Brandeis University, Abraham Maslow, defined five levels of communication.

Our impersonal greetings, "How are you?" and "Have a good day," meant simply to fill an otherwise embarrassing silence, are the first level.

Conversation that makes a third person the subject of conversation is the second level, while on the third level subjects are discussed: politics, sports, the weather. All of these levels are "safe," because the speakers need not reveal their selves. But as we open up and reveal our joys and sorrows, hopes and fears, expectations and anxieties, dreams and dreads, successes and failures, only then do we experience *koinonia*. This is the fourth level. And when our listener responds by sharing how he or she feels, then we have *koinonia* on the fifth level.

This openness, this transparency, this willingness to let others see us as we are, warts and wings, is implied in John's statement: "If we walk in the light, as he [God] is in the light, we have fellowship with one another, and the blood of Jesus his Son cleanses us from all sin" (1 John 1:7). And this type of interchange, so necessary for *koinonia*, applies to our relationship with God as well.

However, the building of a sense of community

is not limited to direct verbal conversation. In *The Lutheran* (Feb. 1, 1978), Mary Jo Emmons describes what Sunday morning worship means to her:

> I listen for Barbara's lilting soprano and Jim's rich bass. As we speak or sing together, we echo each other's prayers and praise. Listen, our voices say to each other, listen to the humanity of which we are a part.

Invisible, unspoken *koinonia* is often experienced at times of stress and sorrow. Mary Jo Emmons continues:

> I went last year to the funeral of a good friend. I had expected to be comforted by the sight of our pastor and the sound of hope and love in his words. I hadn't realized how deeply comforting the simple nearness of my friend's other friends, gathered with me in gentle remembrance, would be.

Koinonia means, not only community, but also partnership. Partnership is *koinonia* in overalls, *koinonia* visible in dollar bills, canned goods, warm blankets, and hours of volunteer time. The New Testament frequently refers to this type of *koinonia*. Paul thanked the Philippians for their *partnership* with him in the gospel through the offerings they had sent (Phil. 1:5).

This is one of the aspects of belonging to a denomination that appeals greatly to me. The little I have to give would be lost in a sea of need, nor would I know where to give it, if I were to give it alone. But by pooling my gift with the gifts of thousands, I can encircle the world: supplying blankets in earthquake-stricken Peru and food in Bangladesh, helping radio the gospel message to China and Russia, sending love and shelter to the orphans of war-torn countries, bringing comfort to the dying. On and on the list goes.

When I link arms in partnership with God's children in the community of a congregation, and even more significantly, in a large church body, my outreach is breathtaking. Life glows with meaning. My horizons are stretched wide, and my love can take wings and fly.

Sometimes the desire to share becomes so consuming and joyous that a person's whole self is poured out for *koinonia*. I think, for example, of the young college student so deeply moved by a class on world hunger that she changed her major and is devoting her life to aquaculture, learning to farm the seas to provide needed protein for the hungry of the world. Her whole life is becoming a symphony of *koinonia*.

Koinonia brings growth. "I learn from my friends," Mary Jo Emmons testifies. "We are a people-in-community, an open, flexible community whose avowed purpose is growth."

Christ Jesus, our Savior and our Lord, has left us an example to follow. He has shared with us and appeals to us. "Give," he says, "and it shall be given unto you."

"Yes," the poet says, "Give, give till the Lord stops giving to you."

Koinonia. Fellowship. Partnership. Community. Unselfish, generous sharing. The spontaneous glad response of members of a family who are "for one another," the family of God.

Let us pray.

Our loving God, at times it is so hard to be "for one another." Help us to remember we are all parts of one body, interdependent with all of those with whom we share life. Erase envy and past hurts, ease tensions, and uplift us to the joy that comes with experiencing true *koinonia*. Amen.

Receive God's blessing.

May the fellowship of the Holy Spirit be with you all. Amen.

leitourgia (lay-tour-GHEE-ah)
service

LITURGY OF SOAPSUDS, GAVELS, AND DOLLAR BILLS

Let us pray.

Master, let me walk with you
In lowly paths of service true;
Tell me your secret; help me bear
The strain of toil, the fret of care.
—Washington Gladden

Our Bible reading is from John 13:1-17.

The meditation

Several years ago a Catholic monk by the name of Brother Lawrence found himself assigned to scour and scrub pots and pans in the kitchen of a monastery. The noisy kitchen stood in strident contrast to the quiet chapel, but Brother Lawrence discovered he could have his own unique liturgical service as the soapsuds flew and the scouring powders wrinkled and reddened his hands.

"The time of business does not differ from the time of prayer," Brother Lawrence wrote, "and in the noise and clutter of my kitchen, while several

83

persons are at the same time calling for different things, I possess God in as great tranquility as if I were upon my knees at the Blessed Sacrament."

In regarding the performance of his daily chores as a worship service, Brother Lawrence had discovered the fullest meaning of *leitourgia* (lay-tour-GHEE-ah). For *leitourgia,* from which we have derived the English word "liturgy," in its widest sense means any service we perform for another.

The word *leitourgia* was not always so expansive in meaning. Originally it was used by the Greeks only when a man voluntarily offered his services to the state, enlisting in military service.

But as time passed, people began to use the word to include also those services which the state *asked* citizens to perform. These services were, in effect, a type of income tax. When a person's income equaled or surpassed a certain sum, the state asked that person to make a specific contribution to the welfare of the state.

These contributions to the state were called *leitourgein* (lay-tour-GAIN). They were given for one of four purposes: (1) to develop art and culture; (2) to train professional athletes; (3) to send ambassadors to neighboring states, either on special missions or to participate in a solemn state celebration; and (4) to support the defense program of the government, especially in times of war.

As the years passed, people began to use the word *leitourgia* even more widely, to include the services of entertainers and even prostitutes! Finally people were using the word to describe the services any person performed for another and also the services a priest performed in the temple.

We find the word *leitourgia* used three ways in the New Testament.

84

Paul used *leitourgia* to describe the service Christians render to one another. When he wrote of the offerings the Christians in Macedonia and Achaia had sent for the poor in Jerusalem, he referred to their gifts as *leitourgein* (Rom. 15:27). When he wrote ahead to the church at Corinth advising them to gather an offering for the poor, he referred to this appeal as a *leitourgia*.

Paul added, "so that it [the gift] may be ready not as an exaction but as a willing gift" (2 Cor. 9:5). This reminds us of the earliest use of the word to denote voluntary service.

Likewise, when Paul wrote a thank-you letter to the Philippians acknowledging with gratitude the gift of money they had sent him, he called their gift a *leitourgia*.

Epaphroditus, the Philippian Christian who carried the cash gift to Paul, stayed on with Paul in Rome, to encourage and cheer him and run errands for him while Paul was in prison. Paul referred to Epaphroditus' service also as *leitourgia*. So we may say when we give our money in offerings and our time in volunteer work we are performing a full liturgical service.

New Testament writers also used the word *leitourgia* to designate the ritualistic service Zechariah performed in the temple (Luke 1:23). When the church laid hands on Paul and Barnabas and set them aside for the work of church-founding and church-building, this calling too was referred to as *leitourgia* (Acts 13:1-3).

Christ's ministry of being a high priest, one who intercedes to God on our behalf, was also called a *leitourgia* (Heb. 8:6). So we may say that, when we worship God in a formal, ritualistic way, when we give ourselves to the particular calling God has for

85

us, and when we pray for others, we are engaged in a full liturgical service.

Also, Paul uses the word *leitourgia* to describe the work of a magistrate (Rom. 13:6). So we may say, when we assume any civic, state, or national responsibility, we are engaging in a full liturgical service.

Finally, the word *leitourgia* came to mean *any* service we perform for another. I wonder if it was from Brother Lawrence that Ruth Bell Graham, Billy Graham's wife, picked up this lesson. I recall years ago reading about a sign Ruth had hung above her kitchen sink: "Three worship services held here daily." That is understanding *leitourgia* in its fullest sense.

For whether it be offerings given, aid or support offered, participation in a worship service, obeying God's call, commissioning and supporting kingdom workers, participating in civic or state affairs, or doing the daily basic chores life demands of us, all of this, done in the name of the Lord Jesus, with thankful hearts, becomes our liturgy of worship to our God.

Let us pray.

O God, great works do not always lie in our way, but every day we may do little ones excellently, that is, with great love. Enable us to regard all work as service rendered gladly unto you. Amen.

—St. Francis de Sales, adapted

Receive God's blessing.

May you go out in joy, and be led forth in peace. May your hearts so vibrate with gladness that it will seem as though even the mountains and hills are breaking forth in song, and the trees of the fields are clapping their hands. May you experience a sense of harmony with your Creator God and his creation and rejoice that you are his. Amen.

THE UNPOPULAR THREE-LETTER WORD

Let us pray.

O God, our Redeemer, give us awareness of your presence, insight into ourselves, humility to acknowledge our needs, willingness to seek your help, trust to believe you will act on our behalf, and thanksgiving for all you intend to do for us. Amen.

Our Bible reading is from Romans 3:23.

The meditation

In his book *Whatever Became of Sin?* Dr. Karl Menninger says, "Sin is an implicit, aggressive quality— a ruthlessness, a hurting, a breaking away from God and the rest of humanity, a partial alienation, or act of rebellion. . . . *Someone* is defied or offended or hurt by sin. . . . Sin is thus, at heart, a refusal of the love of others."

Hamartia (ha-mar-TEE-ah) is the Greek word used most often (more than 60 times in Paul's letters alone) to describe sin. The word originally meant "missing the mark," as when one throws a dart at the bull's-eye and misses.

The Bible is replete with descriptions of how we miss the mark. Let us consider 10 ways we fail as we see them portrayed in the story of David and Bathsheba.

We read in 2 Samuel 11:1: "In the spring of the year, the time when kings go forth to battle, David sent Joab, and his servants [to battle.] . . . But David remained at Jerusalem." The New Testament has raised searching questions about war, but in David's day it was an accepted way of life. A king considered it his duty to accompany his troops to war, and David, in not doing so, was shirking duty. *Adikia* (ah-de-KEE-ah) is what the Bible calls this sin of refusing to give to God and people that which is their just due, considering self more important than others. Possibly David thought, "Why should I risk being killed when I can pay others to take this chance?" Or perhaps he was suffering from middle-age boredom and was looking for something that would give him "kicks."

"It happened," the story continues. *Paraptoma* (pa-RAHP-tom-ah) in English is translated "trespasses," but it carries also the meaning of an unpremeditated slip, as when you accidentally step on a banana peel, which sprawls you on the floor.

David "saw from the roof a woman bathing; and the woman was very beautiful," we read. *Epithumia* (eh-pith-oo-MEE-ah), desire for that which he had no right to—was born in David's heart as he gazed on the woman. The Evil One makes a studied art of learning how to appeal to desire.

"And David sent and inquired about the woman. And one said, 'Is not this Bathsheba . . . the wife of

Uriah the Hittite?' So David sent messengers, and took her; and she came to him, and he lay with her."

We can identify here three different sins. *Pesha* (pah-SHAH) is the Hebrew word meaning deliberately stepping across the line, in this case, deliberately committing adultery when God's law says, "You shall not commit adultery." *Pesha* is both transgression and rebellion, rebellion against a superior. David was guilty of *adikia* also, departure from the moral laws, and *anomia* (ah-no-MEE-ah), thumbing one's nose at God's laws, saying, "So what?"

"And the woman conceived; and she sent and told David, 'I am with child.' So David sent word to Joab, 'Send me Uriah.'"

David wanted to cover his sin, which led him to *apate* (ah-PAH-tay), deceit. He tried unsuccessfully to get Uriah to stay with his wife and make love to her. Soldiers on duty felt they should deny themselves this pleasure, and Uriah refused to be disloyal to his troops.

So frustrated David thought up another device to conceal his sin. He wrote a letter to Joab: "Set Uriah in the forefront of the hardest fighting," David wrote, "and then draw back from him, that he may be struck down, and die." David became guilty of yet another sin: *prosopolepsia* (praw-so-poe-lape-SEE-ah), lack of respect for persons. David considered Uriah expendable if he, David, could accomplish his own ends by getting rid of Uriah.

"Uriah the Hittite was slain." And when David received the news, he sent word to Joab, "Do not let this matter trouble you, for the sword devours now one and now another."

Hebrews 3:13 warns us against letting ourselves become hardened by the deceitfulness of sin. That hardening began taking place in David. Sin deceived him into believing what he did was all right.

"When the wife of Uriah heard that Uriah her husband was dead, she made lamentation for her husband." *Kakia* (kah-KEE-ah), translated "evil," means anything morally bad or wicked, but also anything deliberate that produces or threatens to produce sorrow, distress, or calamity. David brought grief and sorrow to Bathsheba and the family of Uriah.

"But the thing that David had done displeased the Lord. And the Lord sent Nathan to David." In his visit Nathan recounted a story to David of the rich man who took and killed the pet lamb of the poor man in order to make lamb stew for a visitor who dropped in. "David's anger was greatly kindled against the man" who had done this, we read. But Nathan, turning to David, said, "You are the man."

Nathan then reviewed all that God had done for David, and he concluded with, "And if this were too little," the Lord said, "I would add to you as much more." *Opheilema* (oh-FAY-lay-mah) means debts. Though he was indebted to God for all, David was not satisfied with what he had received but instead struck out on his own to gather even more for himself. In his act we see reflected David's failure to trust that God would give him all that he needed and all that was good for him. He wanted to become god for himself, to run his life as he chose.

"Why?" Nathan thunders, "why have you despised the word of the Lord?" *Ephaulisas* (eh-PHAU-lih-sahs) is translated "despised" or "set at naught." Nathan was asking, "Why do you treat God's word as though it doesn't mean anything? Why do you scorn it and treat it with contempt?"

In *Searchlight on Bible Words,* James Hefley tells

the story of Joyce Nies and Esther Matteson. Deep in the jungles of Peru, they wondered why Piro Christians, when reading aloud from the New Testament, frequently would stop reading. Finally one of the men explained: "I will tell you why. . . . When we ourselves have done something evil, and we find it written in God's Word, we are amazed and shocked. We cannot pronounce what we see written, because that is what we have done. It is as though our sins are told right out in the daylight. We are ashamed of what we have done in the eyes of God."

So, too, we squirm as we read the story of David.

For when I, like David, refuse to give to people that which is just and right for them to receive, I am guilty of sin.

When I consider myself more important than others, I am guilty of sin.

When I slip and fall, even if I didn't mean to fall, I am guilty of sin.

When I desire to possess that which it is not right for me to possess, I am guilty of sin.

When I have an insolent, contemptuous attitude toward God's laws, when I depart from them and break them, I am guilty of sin.

When I deceive, I am guilty of sin.

When I consider others expendable so I may achieve success, I am guilty of sin.

When I deliberately do anything that produces sorrow, distress, or calamity for another, I am guilty of sin.

When I act in defiance to God, choosing to become god unto myself, I am guilty of sin.

When I mistrust God's goodness and love, I am guilty of sin.

When I refuse to love others, I am guilty of sin.

When I, like David, put myself in the center of life, I am guilty of sin.

But, thanks be to God, "if we confess our sins, he is faithful and just, and will forgive our sins and cleanse us from all unrighteousness" (1 John 1:9).

Let us pray.

O God, may we thirst thy love to know. Lead us in our sin and woe, to where the healing waters flow. Hear us, holy Jesus. Amen.

—Thomas Benson Pollock

Receive God's blessing.

"The grace of our Lord Jesus Christ and the love of God and the fellowship of the Holy Spirit be with you all" (2 Cor. 13:14). Amen.

THE CHURCH GATHERED TOGETHER

Let us pray.

A multitude comes
    from the east and the west
To sit at the feast of salvation
With Abraham, Isaac,
    and Jacob, the blest,
Obeying the Lord's invitation.
Have mercy upon us, O Jesus! Amen.

—Magnus Brostrup Lanstad

Our Bible reading is from Acts 20:28.

The meditation

Some time ago I was talking with a Russian Christian who, along with his family and aged mother, had been able to emigrate to the United States. He related incident after incident of police breaking up meetings and intimidating Christians so they no longer dared to gather at church.

"When that happened," he said, "we took to meeting in homes. This really wasn't satisfactory because the homes were small, and they became overcrowded. The ventilation was bad, the lighting was bad, and there weren't adequate exits in case of fire. Sometimes because of all this the police came to the homes also and broke up the meetings. Then we Christians had to agree to meet together in small groups. But most of us felt this compulsion to come together. We derived strength to carry on as together we studied the Word and prayed."

We felt this compulsion to come together. Coming together in assembly is intrinsic in the meaning of *ekklesia* (eck-klay-SEE-ah), the word the first Christians chose to identify their gatherings. We translate it "church." Would not the popular little chorus be more theologically correct if it were changed to:

> I'm not the church; you're not the church
> But we're the church together.
> All who follow Jesus, all around the world,
> Yes, we're the church together.

The word *ekklesia* has both a Greek and a Hebrew background. Let us first consider the Greek.

In the city of Athens, Greece, the city government was democratic. Every male citizen who had not lost his civic rights had a right to vote. The *ekklesia* was the assembly of people called together for business.

The assembly wielded sweeping powers. It elected and dismissed magistrates, declared war, made peace, drew up treaties, handled financial affairs, and determined city policies. The assembly also elected generals and other military officers and assigned troops to campaigns and dispatched them.

When the assembly was convened, they began with prayer and sacrifice to their deities. The two watchwords they referred to frequently were equality and freedom.

But the word *ekklesia* had a Hebrew background as well. In the Hebrew it came from a root word meaning "to summon." More than 70 times the word appears in the Septuagint. Referring to the Hebrew background of the word, Barclay has defined the meaning of the *ekklesia* as:

> a body of people, not so much assembling because they have chosen to come together, but assembling because *God has called them to Himself;* not so much assembling to share their own thoughts and opinions but *assembling to listen to the voice of God.*

The New Testament used the word *ekklesia* in three different ways. First, *ekklesia* means the universal church.

When I lived in India we gathered on Sunday evenings for a vesper service. As we sat in church we could hear the temple bells ringing across the valley and the chanting of Tibetan priests nearby. We were a tiny Christian minority in a vast land, and we felt almost swallowed up. How encouraging it was to lift our sights as we sang an evening hymn that underscores the theme of the universal church of Jesus Christ:

> We thank you that your Church, unsleeping
> While earth rolls onward into light,
> Through all the world its watch is keeping,
> And never rests by day or night.
>
> As to each continent and island
> The dawn leads on another day,
> The voice of prayer is never silent,
> Nor dies the strain of praise away.
>
> The sun, here having set, is waking
> Your children under western skies,
> And hour by hour, as day is breaking,
> Fresh hymns of thankful praise arise.
>
> —John Ellerton

96

Ekklesia is also used in the New Testament to mean a particular local church. Paul speaks of "the church of God which is at Corinth" and "the churches of Galatia" (1 Cor. 1:2; Gal. 1:2).

But *ekklesia* also means any group of Christians who meet together to worship. When Paul wrote to the group at Corinth who were getting together for potluck suppers, after which they would celebrate the Lord's Supper, he referred to their coming together as "assembling as a church."

It would seem that as Paul moved along in life and in his ministry he shifted from placing emphasis on the individual groups to the universal church. Sir William Ramsay believes that the prevailing Roman thought of the day probably influenced Paul in this respect. No matter where a Roman citizen went and no matter how long he might live in a country far distant from his native land, still he always was conscious of being a Roman. Down through the centuries the Hebrew people have maintained this same type of consciousness. And it surely is an intrinsic characteristic of Christians. Culture and custom may differentiate us one from the other, but our common faith in Christ unites us, and this unity is felt instantly when one meets another Christian.

I think of the communion service at a leper colony in Africa where we knelt together, African and American, leper and nonleper, and sensed our unity in the Lord Jesus as we shared the elements.

The Marriage Encounter movement, which has brought help and blessing to thousands, emphasizes that every Christian home should house a little church. This is good theology. From there we move on to membership in a local congregation, for as Samuel Johnson observed:

97

> To be of no church is dangerous. Religion, of
> which the rewards are distant, and which is
> animated only by faith and hope, will glide by
> degrees out of the mind, unless it be invigorated
> and reimpressed by external ordinances, by
> stated calls to worship, and the salutary influ-
> ence of example.

It is not wrong to be justly proud of belonging to
a denomination of one's own conviction. But it is
the awareness of being part of the worldwide church
of Jesus Christ that will cheer, encourage, and in-
spire us most of all.

Let us pray.

Lord, lift our sights so we may grow more conscious
of the vast assembly of which we are a part.
Strengthen your church, especially where persecuted
Christians gather for worship. Uphold and save
those who suffer for their faith. May we never take
for granted or cease to be thankful that we can meet
together. In Christ's name. Amen.

Receive God's blessing.

"Now to him who is able to keep you from falling
and to present you without blemish before the presence of his glory with rejoicing, to the only God,
our Savior through Jesus Christ our Lord, be glory,
majesty, dominion, and authority, before all time
and now and for ever. Amen" (Jude 24-25).

WHO WANTS TO BE DIFFERENT?

Let us pray.

The concerns of our daily life clutter our minds, O God. The pull of the world is strong. During these moments of quietness, speak to us. Amen.

Our Bible reading is from Ephesians 1:3-4.

The meditation

One of the adventures of my simple childhood was to spend a night in the home of a friend. I remember one home in particular. Whenever my friend and I climbed the stairs to the second floor, we were always confronted at the top with a closed door. For the longest time I wondered what was behind that door. Finally I asked my friend. She put her finger over her lips, and we tiptoed to the closed door. Up by the top molding she found a key and took it down, slipped it into the lock, and then very quietly opened the door.

Holding our breath, we crept inside and shut the door behind us. I stood blinking. The green shades at the long narrow windows were pulled to the bot-

99

tom, letting in only narrow slats of light. Then I saw the huge bolstered bed, the Victorian lamp with delicate roses painted on it, the intricately carved rocking chair, the ornate, bulky commode. I realized it was only a bedroom. Still, the musty smell and shadowy darkness made it mysterious.

"It's for guests," my friend whispered. "My mother keeps it especially for guests."

It didn't occur to either of us then to call that room a holy room, but if we had, in one sense, we would have named it well. For "holy" as it is used in the Bible means that which is separated or set apart, that which is different. At least that's what the original Greek word, *hagios* (HAH-gee-os), meant, and when biblical writers began to use it, the word took on the added meaning of that which is set apart for God.

Understanding the biblical meaning of "holy" helps us to understand phrases like "a people holy unto God," and "thou shalt keep the Sabbath holy."

Christians should be different—not odd or peculiar, but different from the world in their values, moral code, goals, and manner of life. Too often we blend with the world, and people see no difference in us. Too often, instead of trailblazing, we follow two steps behind. We use the same current vocabulary, follow the same trends, and even repeat the same teachings as non-Christians, only tacking on little moralistic paragraphs at the end. Few dare to be different. It takes courage to be different.

In a nearby high school every year an "I Dare" Award is given to a young person whom teachers feel has courage and conviction for independent thought and action. Many of the students do not consider this honor to be desirable, however, because the person who wins it is often ridiculed for being different. Although I do not wish anyone the pain of rejection and ridicule, I always am pleased when a Christian young person is granted the award. If we were living *hagios* lives, we all would be recipients of the "I Dare" Award, but too often we shrink from being different.

Peter wrote: "As obedient children . . . be holy in all you do" (1 Peter 1:15 NIV). Paul added: "Don't let the world around you squeeze you into its own mold" (Rom. 12:2 Phillips). The Living Bible states: "I plead with you to give your bodies to God. Let them be a living sacrifice, holy—the kind he can accept. . . . Don't copy the behavior and customs of this world, but be a new and different person with a fresh newness in all you do and think" (Rom. 12:1-2).

In response to our thoughtless remark, "Who wants to be different?" Paul asks this penetrating question: "When you think of what [Jesus] has done for you, is this too much to ask?" Then he adds a promise: "Be a new and different person. . . . Then you will learn from your own experience how his ways will really satisfy you" (Rom. 12:1-2 LB).

Let us pray.

O God, our source of strength, give us the courage to be different when loyalty to you and your Word demands that we be different. Amen.

Receive God's blessing.

May God grant you growth in grace and holiness. Amen.

A TOP-NOTCH UMPIRE

Let us pray.

O God,
Breathe through the heats
of our desire
Thy coolness and thy balm;
Let sense be dumb; let flesh retire;
Speak through the earthquake,
wind, and fire,
O still small voice of calm! Amen.

—John Greenleaf Whittier

Our Bible reading is from John 14:27.

The meditation

A recent issue of the *Reader's Digest* recounts this incident:

> The scene: Boston Garden, tightly packed for the fifth game in the 1976 National Basketball Association championship series. A high-leaping Boston Celtic player swishes the ball through the basket, and the buzzer sounds to end the second overtime period—and the game. Bedlam erupts as the hometown fans cheer a Celtic victory over the Phoenix Suns.
>
> But a sweat-drenched referee, Richie Powers, views the game more precisely. The timekeeper, he notices, failed to stop the clock after the goal,

so Powers rules that there is one second left in the game. When the clock starts again, the score is 112-110 in favor of Boston, but in that one second the Suns tie the game and send it into a third overtime period. Now the hometown fans feel like killing Powers. One woman throws her purse at him and screams: "You ain't even human!" (from "Referee: Roughest Role in Sports" by Bill Surface, December 1976).

Sports professionals consider the job of an umpire or referee the most difficult in all of professional basketball, baseball, football, and hockey. Not only must an umpire be physically fit and strong, possess superior vision, be able to remember over 100 pages of rules, and make snap decisions, but he also must be able to retain composure in the face of hurled ice, frankfurters, bottles, and jeers.

Christians are not exempt from deeply felt emotions which so stir us that we cannot think objectively and reasonably. In situations that produce anxiety and when conflicting views wound and separate. God has given us an umpire. Paul declares, "Let the peace of Christ rule in your hearts, to which indeed you were called in the one body" (Col. 3:15). The Greek word for "let it rule" is *brabeueto* (brah-bew-EH-toe), and from it came the name given to the men who did the official ruling for the Olympics, the umpires.

Let us consider the peace of God, which Paul declares can act as umpire for us in emotionally charged situations.

What are the characteristics of this umpire? The peace of God, first of all, has its roots in a relationship that is right with God, when hostilities between God and us have ceased.

When we first came to East Africa, our curiosity was aroused by the way the Africans shook hands.

103

They placed their left hand on their right forearm before extending their right hand. One day I asked an African friend the reason for this. He smiled.

"Oh, that," he said. "That's a carry-over from the olden days when Africa was a continent of thousands of tribes, each tribe suspicious of all others. So if you wanted to reassure a stranger that you were a friend and not an enemy, you would shake hands in this way, proving that you were not clasping a knife or a spear behind your back with your left hand."

God offers his hand to us with his left hand on his right forearm. He grasps no weapon behind his back with which to stab us, for Christ has made peace through his blood. If there is hostility between God and us now, the hostility is on our part. When *we* cease our hostilities toward God, when we quit being angry with, quarreling with, or mistrusting God, when we decide to shake hands with him, then we experience what it means to be at peace with God.

We need to remember, however, that it is possible to have peace with God only because God, in his love, had mercy on us and gave us his Son to die for us. The first Christians understood this. When they greeted each other, they not only said, "Peace!" but "Grace and peace" or "Grace, mercy, and peace." So then, the peace of God can serve as our umpire only when we first have come into a peaceful relationship with God.

Being at peace with God does not depend on our feelings. At the same time, when we make our relationship with God our continuing home, we begin to experience the peace *of* God. This peace is an emotion which comes from God himself, an emotion we can experience and enjoy in spite of circumstances. "Peace I leave with you," Jesus said. "My peace I give to you; not as the world gives do I give to you" (John 14:27).

A friend of mine lay in the hospital dying of cancer. "I should be fearful and worried and sad, I would think," she said. "But instead I have the most wonderful peace within my heart. It must be that peace which passes understanding that I've read about in the Bible."

The peace of God, which can act as our umpire, is also a felt emotion of calmness and reassurance and quiet conviction. This peace can umpire in sticky, emotionally charged situations where differences of opinion threaten to split and divide. Congregations, church councils, committees, and various other groups sometimes find themselves thrust into these painful, disturbing situations. When this happens, we do well to remind ourselves to wait until the peace of God can calm and quiet our excited hearts and minds. When passion is aroused, reason suffers, and, as is commonly expressed, more heat is generated than light. God's peace needs to reign, to act as our umpire, so we shall not do that which is wrong. When we are quiet and calm, we shall be able to hear our Umpire calling to tell us whether an action is fair play or foul.

This does not mean, however, that our decisions necessarily will guarantee favorable reception by all. Our decisions might provoke jeers, misunderstanding, and anger, as is true in sports events. Sometimes, unfortunately, it seems that splits are inevitable. But when decisions are made in an atmosphere where the peace of God has reigned, we shall be able to listen to questions and accusations without being moved, even though our hearts may be troubled by the pain all have suffered.

So, then, in the first place, we understand that the

peace of God, which is to be our umpire, is a gift from God, possessed only by those who have made peace with God. In the second place, the peace of God is a calming emotion in the midst of upset. And, in the third place, we are to let that peace of God to be our umpire and allow it to take control. Then we shall be able to continue to live and walk in peace and love.

Let us pray.

O God, make us children of quietness and heirs of peace. Amen.   —St. Clement

Receive God's blessing.

"The peace of God, which transcends human under-standing, will keep constant guard over your hearts and minds as they rest in Christ Jesus" (Phil. 4:7, Phillips). Amen.

BURNED OUT

Let us pray.

Eternal One, help us for just a few minutes to shut out all wandering thoughts and concentrate instead on you. Amen.

Our Bible reading is from Revelation 2:2-5.

The meditation

Rev. J. Russell Hale, professor of church and society at Lutheran Theological Seminary, Gettysburg, Pa., decided to try to find out why 80 million people in America have nothing whatsoever to do with organized religion. His research carried him 30,000 miles.

After 165 interviews, Rev. Hale made eight classifications: True Unbelievers, Publicans, the Boxed-In, the Locked-Out, Nomads, Anti-Institutionalists, Pilgrims, and Burned-Outs. The Burned-Outs were those once heavily involved in church work who tired of it or decided it consumed too much time and money. "You get bombarded," one said.

Somehow the writers of the New Testament did not seem to believe that you could get "too involved" or work too hard for God. Rather, both the Lord Jesus and the apostle Paul spoke of working so hard in God's service that it could be described only as

107

"toil," or as the Greek word, *kopos* (KOH-poes), describes it, "toil to the point of sweat." "I worked harder than any of them [the apostles]," Paul declares in 1 Corinthians 15:10.

In Galatians 4:11 Paul fleetingly wonders if his labor has been worthwhile, because some Christians were slipping back into old ways. Paul laments, "I am afraid I have labored over you in vain." Paul often refers to the Christians as his children, so perhaps the labor Paul is thinking of here is the travail of a woman giving birth to a child. Women who have been conscious throughout the entire birth process will tell you that they have never worked so hard before or since. It is labor to the point of grunting and straining, of perspiring and biting one's lips in order not to cry out against the pain as muscles stretch in unwonted ways.

The early church listed by name some who had labored for the Lord: Tryphaena, Tryphosa, Persis. Their labor is described as toil, long, exhausting labor, producing weariness (Rom. 16:12). Our Risen Lord, in his opening remarks to the Christians at Ephesus, says, "I know your works, your toil" (Rev. 2:2). Few of us, even though we might claim to having been "burned out," have labored in God's kingdom to the extent that we can truly classify it as grunting, sweating, expending-every-effort, bringing-to-birth labor.

The Ephesian Christians had toiled in this way. Sadly enough, though, it would appear that they also had become "burned out." The Lord warns them, "Think where you were before you fell; repent, and do as you used to at first, or else, if you will not repent, I shall come to you and take your lamp-stand from its place" (Rev. 2:5 JB). Solemn words those.

108

Our Lord also hints at the cause of their having burned out. "You have less love now than you used to" (Rev. 2:4 JB).

What then is the secret of continuing to love? What is the secret of not burning out?

Our Lord himself pointed the way. "Come to me," he invites, "all you who labor and are overburdened, and I will give you rest" (Matt. 11:28 JB). Today's English Bible translates this verse: "Come to me, all of you who are tired from carrying your heavy loads, and I will give you rest."

If we burn out, it could be because we have allowed our labor to become so time- and energy-consuming and burdensome that we have stopped coming to Jesus for renewal. We need to meet him face to face, to let the loads under which we sweat and moan and groan slip from our shoulders to rest in his arms. "The busier I am," Luther used to say, "the more time I need to spend in prayer." Wise man! He knew the secret of not burning out, even though he was one who labored more abundantly than all the others.

In his invitation Jesus continues, "My yoke is easy, and my burden is light." The picture is of the wooden yoke that slips over the necks of a team of oxen. The meaning of "easy" is "fits well." So Jesus is saying, "Rest assured, the task, the burden I give you, the job I give you, will fit you well, and furthermore, we shall bear it together, you and I. Because I bear it with you, your burden shall be light."

If our work for God is burdensome, it could be because it is something *we* have chosen, not a commission *God* has given to us. Or it could be that we are striving to do it by ourselves, with our own strength. If this is so, we most surely will burn out.

109

But we need not, for God has made every provision for us.

> So, labor on. Spend and be spent!
>   Thy joy to do the Father's will.
> It is the way the Master went;
>   Should not the servant tread it still?
>
> —Horatius Bonar

Only remember as you labor for the Eternal One: let him choose the task for you and bear the burden with you, and keep coming back to him for renewal.

Let us pray.

O God, our Sustainer, keep us from fainting on the way and becoming discouraged. Refresh and strengthen us in Christ's name. Amen.

Receive God's blessing.

May the Lord provide for your every need as you wait for him. May he be the strong arm you can lean on every morning, the one who comes to your side at a time of trouble. May he give you double portions of wholeness, wisdom, and weathering ability. Amen.

analuein (ah-naw-LOO-ane)
to pull up anchor; to pull up stakes
sunechomai (soon-EK-oh-my)
I am hard-pressed; I am compressed

CAUGHT IN A SQUEEZE

Let us pray.

Dear God, save us from making easy decisions when we are caught in difficult situations. Amen.

Our Bible reading is from Philippians 1:22-25.

The meditation

In a day of instant foods, instant production of copies, and instant relief from pain, endurance and perseverance are in short order. When things don't go our way, we quickly become irked and dissatisfied.

How different for the apostle Paul. Old age found him under house arrest in Rome. He didn't know what the future held, whether he would live or die. And if he lived, he did not know what lay ahead for him. Already he had endured so much. Red welts and raised stripes crisscrossed his broken body, mute testimonies to beatings and whiplashings. At night when he could not sleep, he was haunted by memories of stonings, hunger, gossip, wounding criticism,

111

backbiting, jealousy, envy, misunderstanding, and seasick, perilous days on the waters.

Christ meant everything to Paul. Over and over he declared that there could be nothing better than to be with Christ. Christ was that real to him. But we also see a natural human survival instinct when Paul cries out to his friends at Philippi: "If I could choose to live or die, which would I do? I find the choice so difficult, it's like being compressed, *sunechomai* (soon-EK-oh-my), like being caught in a narrow, rocky crevasse through which I can barely squeeze, so narrow I can't turn around. Life's problems are so complex and perplexing that, of course, I'd rather *analuein* (an-naw-LOO-ane), pull up the stakes, fold up my little tent, and move on. I would rather loosen the mooring ropes, pull up the anchor, and set sail. But I know you need me, and so, if God wills it, I'll hang on. For your sakes I'll choose to live."

And that resolve Paul made even if it meant more beatings and more stonings.

Has life presented you with circumstances so painful and perplexing that you wish you could die and go to be with the Lord? Do you sometimes feel your church is so dead you would like to move on to where there appears to be life and vigor? Is it so difficult to be a Christian at your job that you dream of finding an easier place to work? Are your parents so unable to understand you that you wish you could find another place to live? Is life with your spouse so unbearable you are tempted to walk out? Are your children so self-centered, unappreciative, and demanding you wish you could sweep them all out the door? Is there so much bickering and nit-picking among some of the Christians you know that you're tempted to disassociate yourself from them?

But instead of thinking only of your own comfort, have you thought about whether others need you where you are? If you moved away, could they receive the help they need?

"Because I know you need me, I'm willing to stay on, to continue to live," Paul assured the Philippians. Can that be your response too?

Let us pray.

O God, strengthen us when we falter. Help us not to grow weary and give up. Help us to think not only of our own comfort and profit but also of others' needs. Help us to seek to give rather than to receive. Help us to be patient and wait when results are slow coming, to focus, not on large numbers and huge successes, but rather on loyalty and faithfulness. Amen.

Receive God's blessing.

May the Lord support you all the days of your troubled life, until the shadows lengthen and the evening comes and the fever of life is over. Amen.

ARE YOU A BABY CHRISTIAN?

Let us pray.

Lord Jesus, we thank you that you invite all who are weary and burdened to come to you. We are tired. There are many demands on us. You know the anxieties, the fears, and the guilt of our hearts; the tense muscles, the weary spirits, and the spent resources of our minds. We thank you for the warm acceptance of family and friends who love us. We thank you for your grace and love, which forgive, cleanse, and restore us. Be with us and guide us as we meet together. Amen.

Our Bible reading is from Romans 8:14.

The meditation

A drunken driver ran head-on into a car carrying a young father and mother to a dinner engagement, killing them instantly. Their three little children, at home with a baby-sitter, became orphans. The parents thoughtfully had provided for their little girls through insurance policies. Each child will receive a monthly sum until she comes of age. At

114

that point a substantial sum will be transferred to her personal bank account, and she can draw from it as she wishes. She will no longer be considered a child but a young adult.

The Greek language employs a number of words for "child." *Paidion* (pie-DEE-on) means a little child or infant. *Teknon* (TECK-non) means simply "child," emphasizing the fact of birth. *Huios* (hwee-OS), usually translated "son," emphasizes the dignity and privileges of that role. *Huios* also implies that the behavior and character of the son has become like that of his father.

The word "sons" that Paul used in Romans 8:14 was *huios*. "All who are moved by the Spirit of God are sons of God" (NEB). "For all who are led by the Spirit of God are sons of God" (RSV).

Paul is saying: When you mature enough in your faith so you can trust God to run your life, when you become willing to let the Holy Spirit move you, then it is evident that you have become a *huios*. The inheritance or riches God has for you will be transferred to your account. You may begin to cash in on them, spend them, or invest them. You trust God enough to let him get into the driver's seat of your car and take you where he will. This trust qualifies you to begin to draw from the inheritance God has for you. Your trustful surrender indicates to him that your character and your behavior are harmonious with his.

In your relationship to God, what kind of a child are you? A *paidion*, a little child just learning to walk and feed herself? A *teknon*, who runs carefree and whiles away the day at play? Or are you a *huios*, thinking seriously about life, willing to surrender yourself to God, to let God plan your hours, days, and years? If you are willing to be led by, to be moved by the Spirit of God, Paul says, then you may begin to use the inheritance God has for you. Draw from it. Do not leave it in the heavenly bank and continue to live as a poor person. The riches of God have been transferred to your account. Now write the checks.

Let us pray.

Our loving Savior and Lord, deepen our trust in you so we gladly place ourselves and our future in your hands. Give us courage to ask you to lead us every day. Transform our hearts so we want to do what you want us to do. Help us surrender to you, allowing ourselves to be moved by the Holy Spirit. And then awaken us to the riches that are ours for the asking. Forgive us for living impoverished lives. Help us as mature sons and daughters to claim the inheritance we have in you. Amen.

Receive God's blessing.

Now may God give you courage and boldness to use the gifts he has given you, that we all may come together to oneness of our faith and knowledge of the Son of God and become mature persons, attaining finally the height of full Christian stature. Amen.

NOISY CHATTER OR INTELLIGENT PREACHING?

Let us pray.

Lord, help me to be teachable and receptive. Amen.

Our Bible reading is from Acts 2:17.

The meditation

Capernaum was hot. I sat down under a tree on a fallen, broken piece of a column of the excavated synagogue standing before us. Our Israeli guide sat down before me. His eyes followed mine as they focused on the outside steps of the ancient synagogue. The steps led to a balcony overlooking the main meeting room below.

"You are wondering about those steps?" our guide asked.

I nodded.

"They were for the women. The women entered from outside and went directly to the balcony to sit. Sometimes the balconies were curtained off from the meeting room below, where only men were al-

117

lowed to gather." He paused. "Can you picture it?"

I nodded again.

"All right. Go a step farther. The synagogue is full. The meeting begins. A speaker arises to address the group below. Discussion follows. The women in the balcony lean forward. They can't hear well, or they disagree with what they hear. Excitedly they begin to talk with one another. Soon their voices fill the synagogue. Finally a man below jumps up and calls out: 'Silence! We can't hear ourselves with all your chattering up there.'

" 'We have some questions,' one of the women is brave enough to say.

" 'Then ask your husbands at home!' the retort is given. Quiet takes over—disgruntled quiet, perhaps. The men below continue their discussion. Now that," our guide said, "is what we understand to be the meaning of Paul's words in 1 Corinthians 14:34-35: 'The women should keep silence in the churches. For they are not permitted to speak, but should be subordinate, as even the law says. If there is anything they desire to know, let them ask their husbands at home. For it is shameful for a woman to speak in church.' "

I questioned Luverne that evening when we returned to our hotel. "He's probably right," he said. "The Greek word for 'speak' in the passage in 1 Corinthians is *lalein* (lah-LANE). Another Greek word for 'speak' is *legein* (LEH-gain). *Lalein* was used to describe, not only the noises a human makes, but also thunder rumbling, birds chirping, flies buzzing, or trumpets trumpeting. It was an onomatopoeic word.

"Now the word *legein* means to speak clearly, intelligibly, and with authority. That verb, used often in Revelation, has been translated, 'Thus says

118

the Lord.' It carries the connotation of 'Listen! I have something important to say.' "

Luverne continued: "From many other passages in the New Testament it is clear that in the early church women were free to pray, witness, exhort, and even prophesy, which we understand to mean 'preach.' The Holy Spirit was given to both men and women. Philip had four preacher daughters, and the long list of Christian workers in Romans 16 includes the names of many women."

"Maybe," I ventured, "Capernaum has two lessons for me. One is, I am free to speak, teach, and even preach in church, but," and I grinned, "what I say better be clear, intelligible, backed by the authority of God's Word, and not just chatter."

Let us pray.

Lord, speech is a gift, a privilege, but also a responsibility. Help us to speak words that are true, not deceitful; words that are kind, not harsh; words that build up, not tear down; words that impart wisdom instead of provoking argument; words that cheer, not discourage. Give us courage to speak when we should, even if we would rather remain silent. May our words reflect truly what we believe in and seek to follow. Give us your Spirit in special measure when we speak in a meeting, counsel a friend, or advise a family member. In Jesus' name. Amen.

Receive God's blessing.

Now may the God of peace and order help you not to neglect the gift given you in speech. May he give you wisdom to speak agreeably, with a flavor of wit, learning how to fit your answers to the needs of everyone. Amen.

splanchnizesthai
(splahnk-NID-zes-thigh)
to be moved with compassion

PAIN IN
THE GUT

Let us pray.

O Lord Jesus Christ, the Good Shepherd of the sheep, who came to seek the lost and to gather them into your fold, have compassion upon those who have wandered from you; feed those who hunger, cause the weary to lie down in your pastures, bind up those who are broken in heart, and strengthen those who are weak, that we, relying on your care and being comforted by your love, may abide in your guidance to our lives' end. Amen.

—Sixth-Century Collect

Our Bible reading is from Hebrews 4:15.

The meditation

In *Searchlight on Bible Words,* James Hefley tells the story of Wycliffe workers Bob and Helen Eastman. They were translating Mark 5:19, 6:34, and 9:22 into the language of the Iquito Indians of eastern Peru, and they found themselves searching for a word for "compassion."

"Suppose," Bob asked Felix, their Indian colleague, "suppose the mother in a home dies. After a few days all the food is gone. The children cry. They fall sick. They cling to their father and beg him to help. What would the father say?"

Felix shrugged. "He would say, 'Let them die.'"

Bob opened his mouth, then shut it again. After a few moments of silence he asked, "Would that be right for him to say?"

Felix shrugged again. "Why not?"

"How would he feel?" Bob pursued his search.

Felix thought. "Sad perhaps."

As the Eastmans learned to know the Iquito Indians better, they began to understand what Felix had said. Barely able to keep alive under the conditions of pitiful poverty, the Iquito Indians had been schooled not to care.

In the course of time Felix became a follower of the Suffering Savior.

An epidemic of whooping cough gripped the village. Bob stepped outside his hut one day to find Felix standing there.

"Take this," Felix urged, pressing money into Bob's hands. "Buy medicine for the babies."

Bob stared at the money and then at Felix. Felix smiled.

"Once I didn't know the true road," he confessed. "I lived like a person sleeping. But now I understand."

The Greeks of Jesus' day did not know what it was to have a god who cared. The gods they worshiped held themselves aloof from distressed humanity. So distant were they that they could not be touched by the pitiful cries for help that rose from the throats of the suffering.

Onto this scene strode the strong, virile Son of God. Vigorous in health, commanding in appearance, radiating charisma, he surprised people by his humanity. "He had compassion," we read over and over.

He saw people hungry. "Feed them!" he cried to his followers.

"Let them take care of themselves," his disciples said. "They should have thought ahead and brought their brown bags."

"But they didn't," Jesus said. And he fed them.

He sorrowed with the widow following the bier of her son to the cemetery. The leper, the outcast, the blind stirred up deep pity within his heart.

"Who sinned?" asked his followers, "these who are ill or their parents?" making human misery a theological question to be discussed.

"Neither!" Jesus cried out. "But God desires to see glory come out of even their misery."

The "lostness" of people wandering here and there, bumbling through life without anyone to show them the way, stirred Christ to the depths. "Pray for them!" he cried out. "Ask God to send someone to show them the way. I don't want them lost!"

What an extraordinary god this was, the Greeks said, shaking their heads. This god was moved with compassion.

Splanchnizesthai (splahnk-NID-zes-thigh) is the Greek word for compassion, derived from *splanchna* (SPLANK-na). The *splanchna* were the vital organs: the heart, the lungs, the liver—and the intestines. "To feel at gut level," we say. To be so upset we might have diarrhea or be nauseated. "To have a nail in the heart," the Chol Indians of southern Mexico say.

Jesus relieved the suffering masses of their burdens. The hungry he fed. The sorrowing he comforted. The ill he healed. The lost he led.

We have a God who feels compassion, who is moved by suffering. Are we?

Let us pray.

Our God, there are so many people in the world who suffer injustice, hunger, unemployment, sickness, and despair. Fill us with compassion for all people so we may not only speak compassionately but also act compassionately. Give us courage, strength, and wisdom to work with the vision of a better world for all humanity. Amen.

Receive God's blessing.

May he who bore our griefs and carried our sorrows enable you to take your share of suffering as a good soldier of Christ Jesus. Amen.

GOD TAMES HIS WILD MUSTANG

Let us pray.

O God, our Guide, make us kindly in thought, gentle in word, generous in deed, and true to our convictions. Amen.

Our Bible reading is from Matthew 11:28-30.

The meditation

How would you define meekness? Our English dictionary defines it as "enduring injury with patience and without resentment; deficient in spirit and courage; not violent or strong, moderate."

The Greek word *praotēs* (praw-OH-tase), translated "meek," is a word rich in meaning, defying accurate translation into any one English word. Translators have rendered it "meek," "gentle," and "humble." All these words are applicable, but none adequately expresses what *praotēs* really is. Let us grapple with this elusive Greek word and see if we can grasp at least some of its meaning.

Praotēs or meekness is *not* spinelessness. It is *not* being deficient in spirit and courage. A person may possess the quality of *praotēs* and still churn with anger when injustice is done to others. The anger

124

may even be so keen that it drives the person to work for change.

In Christ's time, High Priest Annas and company were fleecing the common people of about $250,000 a year by the rate they gave in their exchange of money and also by selling, at huge profit, animals and birds for sacrifices. When Jesus learned about this, he was angry—very, very angry. He took radical action to bring about change. He used the whip. Yet Jesus declared he was meek!

But let us note that *praotēs* does not allow for revenge-taking anger because of personal insults or injuries. Jesus showed the appropriate response to personal injury by calling Judas, who betrayed him, "Friend," and by praying that the Father would forgive those who killed him.

Praotēs is the quality of people who allow the Holy Spirit to control and discipline them. *Praus*, from which *praotēs* is derived, suggests a spirited wild horse that has been tamed by his master.

How necessary this taming is we can see in the life of Moses, who in later life was described as being "very meek, meek above all the people on the earth." Born an Israelite, Moses was adopted as a baby by one of the Egyptian princesses. But as he grew to manhood and struggled for identity, Moses could not divorce himself from his own people living in bondage under the Egyptians. Anger smoldered within his heart at the injustices being heaped on them. One day, when he saw an Egyptian beating up on an Israelite, his anger boiled over. He murdered the Egyptian.

Moses was justifiably angry, but he had not yet learned to let God take control, both of himself and of situations. Moses was still the spirited, wild, independent colt, rearing up and hurting, not only himself, but others. As a result, the time when Moses would become leader for his people had to be postponed for several years. God had to tame his wild mustang.

Moses learned to let God control him. He learned to brave Pharaoh's wrath and seek an audience with him. He learned to keep a grumbling, discontented mass of people from revolting. He learned patience in desert wanderings, and he learned to persevere in faith when all seemed hopeless.

I wonder how often Moses longed to be free from the exacting demands of leadership. But God had spoken out of the burning bush, and Moses could not escape that call. When Moses turned himself over to God, God picked up the reins and began to tame him.

In Ephesians 4 we find meekness linked with patience. Paul writes: "Lead a life worthy of the calling to which you have been called, with all lowliness and meekness, with patience."

Moses was a lifetime learning to practice the counsel of Psalm 37:

> Be still before the Lord, and wait patiently for
> him;
> Refrain from anger, and forsake wrath!
> Fret not yourself; it tends only to evil.
> But the meek will possess the land,
> and delight themselves in abundant prosperity
> (vv. 7, 8, 11).

Moses could be patient only because he believed God was in ultimate control.

Humility, too, is an integral part of *praotēs* or meekness. Even Moses was a long time learning true humility. Many long years after Moses murdered the Egyptian, God confronted him. We find Moses now approaching God humbly, but his humility has swung to an extreme. When God says, "Moses, I want you to lead my people out of bondage," Moses replies, "I could never do that!"

True humility is not debasing oneself or speaking disparagingly of one's abilities and gifts, which only calls attention to oneself. True humility is freedom not to be concerned about self at all. When we're truly humble, we know ourselves in our strengths as well as our weaknesses. Moses did not learn to accept fully his strengths; God had to call in Aaron as Moses' assistant, and what a thorn Aaron proved to be to Moses! But Moses did reveal humility in his concern for the integrity of God. This concern dominated his life more than concern for personal safety and popularity, and this motivated Moses to obey God.

Our final point is simply that meekness is learned. "Learn of me," Jesus said. "I am meek and lowly of heart." Only as we are teachable will God be able to train and discipline us so that our strong emotions will not cause us to do and say things we shall regret later. Instead those strong emotions will energize us to act in order to effect change.

So then, in summary, *praotēs*, or meekness, allows for justifiable anger, but does not allow for revenge-taking anger because of personal injuries. *Praotēs* is letting the Holy Spirit take control. *Praotēs* calls for patience. It grows in the soil of humility, and is learned from Jesus.

What does all this mean to me? Simply this. As Christians we are charged to "show meekness toward all men" (Titus 3:2); we are urged to "follow meekness" (1 Tim. 6:11 KJV); to be meek toward those who oppose us (2 Tim. 2:25); "to receive with meekness the implanted word" (James 1:21). And wives are exhorted to put on the imperishable qual-

127

ity of a meek spirit (1 Peter 3:4). How can we obey these exhortations if we don't understand what meekness is?

Let us pray.

Renew Thine image, Lord, in me,
Lowly and gentle may I be;
　No charms but these to Thee are dear;
No anger may'st Thou ever find,
No pride, in my unruffled mind,
　But faith, and heaven-born peace be there.

A patient, a victorious mind,
That life and all things casts behind,
　Springs forth obedient to Thy call,
A heart that no desire can move,
But still to praise, believe, and love,
　Give me, my Lord, my Life, my All!

　　　　　—Johann Anastasius Freylinghausen

Receive God's blessing.

Peace to all of you who are in Christ. Amen.

HANGING IN

Let us pray.

Holy Spirit, capture our wandering thoughts. Clear our minds of the distractions of the day and enable us to hear you speaking to us. Amen.

Our Bible reading is from James 5:7-8, 10-12.

The meditation

On July 3, 1970, when my brother Carl went to bed, he had no premonition that within 24 hours both his arms would be dangling uselessly by his sides. Weeks of pain followed. Carl lost 25 pounds and his arms dropped out of their sockets. The final diagnosis: acute bilateral brachial plexitis, a rare nerve disease for which there is no medication and no known cure.

During months of painful therapy, Carl very slowly regained use of his right hand and arm. The left arm, even today, is weaker, but it can be used in a supportive role.

"How can you be so patient?" I asked Carl one day.

He smiled his slow deliberate smile and said, "You forget that as a farmer I've had many opportunities to grow in faith and trust. I've learned to accept disappointments, failures, illnesses, and setbacks

129

and still carry on. A farmer plows, harrows, fertilizes, kills weeds, plants, cultivates, sprays for insects, and waits for the harvest. A dozen things can happen to rob him of his harvest. If his harvest is destroyed or the yield is only a fraction of what he had hoped for, he doesn't give up farming. He waits until spring and sows again in hope. He hangs in."

Makrothumia (mah-crow-thew-ME-ah) is the Greek word we translate as "patience" or "long-suffering." The word is used in the first book of Maccabees where Rome's supremacy in the world is ascribed to "policy and patience." Rome would never accept defeat and never give in, but persevered.

Rome knew the value of perseverance. Farmers know the value of perseverance. Researchers in science and medicine know the value of perseverance. They know that persevering is the only way discoveries will be made, and that often their work must be a cooperative venture, carried on over a span of years.

In *Forerunners to Everest* René Dittert writes:

> One man prepares the terrain for another. Everywhere, in every field of endeavor, the inaccessible and impossible are only a matter of great patience. It is a patience which man has within him, not as his own property (in fact, failure deprives him of the benefits of his patience), but as a magic ring which the vanquished gives to him who succeeds in the attempt. Thus in the long run, the gates open which man at first believed to be remorselessly closed.

Paul refers to this process when he writes: "I planted, Apollos watered, but God gave the growth" (1 Cor. 3:6).

Makrothumia, as it is used in the New Testament, carries a second meaning also. It is a combination

130

of *thumoi* (thew-MOY), meaning "to flare up in rage," and *makros* (mah-KROSS), meaning "long," and thus we get "long-tempered." *Makrothumia* is the patience or long-suffering that refuses to retaliate even when it is possible to do so.

I remember one day sitting in our Landrover in the Tsavo Wild Animal Game Park in Kenya watching a pride of lions. The cubs were climbing all over the mamas and papas, poking paws into eyes, chewing ears, and just generally being nuisances. The old lions, stretched out on the ground, trying to sleep, bore with it patiently. Occasionally one would raise a paw and push a cub aside, as we would brush an annoying fly away from our face. I marveled. I knew that with one swift sweep of a mighty paw a little cub could be ripped open. But the old lions were patient with their young. Perhaps in their own lion way they understood that the cubs would one day grow up.

It is such patience with the irritating and annoying things people do to us to which *makrothumia* refers. For example, an elderly person receives a phone call, asking if she will be present at the stewardship dinner at church.

"I would like to," the woman replies, "but my failing eyesight doesn't allow me to drive at night."

"Thanks," says the volunteer caller, and she hangs up.

Rebuffed, the woman can feel hurt and sulk and even decide to quit coming to church. Or she can bear patiently with the insults of the thoughtless and phone the church office to ask if anyone could give her a ride.

Makrothumia is Jesus commanding Peter to put away his sword the night Jesus was captured in the garden. It is Jesus standing silent before his taunting accusers. It is the parent keeping the door open for the runaway child. *Makrothumia* is the way God deals with us.

The story is told of Cardinal Mercier, a Belgian cardinal who was in Rome at the time his city, Louvain, was bombed during World War II. Slowly the news filtered through. One-sixth of the city gone. The nave of Mercier's own cathedral a mass of debris. The priceless books of the library of his institute burned. His own home blown to bits. And finally the news that his theological students had been cremated alive.

The Cardinal, torn by anger and grief, roared and ranted. Then suddenly he grew still. His colleagues saw him staring at a small crucifix on the wall. As he turned from the crucifix, tears were streaming down his cheeks.

"A disciple is not above his master," he said. "We will rebuild!"

Makrothumia, one of the indications of being filled with the Spirit, is one of the most critical characteristics for Christian workers to possess. It is the steadfast spirit that will not give in, that can meet disappointments and setbacks and carry on, that can wait for results. Also the humble spirit that can accept insults and injuries without striking back. Without this characteristic the Christian worker will become pessimistic, irritable, cynical, and may even despair to the point of quitting. Without this characteristic, retaliation in one of its most extreme forms, litigation, will increase even among church members and churches.

Makrothumia is in short order these days. It is a lesson we need to learn from our Redeemer who is so patient with us.

132

Let us pray.

Lord, give us a faith that will endure. Amen.

Receive God's blessing.

May the Lord touch your tired body and infuse new life into it. May he make steady your wobbly knees. May your discouragement disappear as you hear him say, "Be strong, and don't be afraid." May your hope be renewed, so you will be able to rise on wings like eagles, to run and not get weary, to walk and not faint. Amen.

baros (BAH-russ)   burden

phortion (for-TEE-on)   burden

TOGETHER AND ALONE

Let us pray.

Give us, O God, love that answers calls for help, sensitivity to see those who are hurting, and wisdom to know how to help. Purify our motives. Help us to serve you with joy. Amen.

Our Bible reading is from Galatians 6:2-5.

The meditation

I sloshed through the rain along a rocky Himalayan trail. I was weary and weak, having just suffered through a bout of amoebic dysentery (an internal landslide, as my mountain friends describe the malady). An emergency had summoned me to the town of Darjeeling 15 miles away. Rain ran down my forehead and into my eyes. My clothing was soaked, and with each step my feet went squish inside my wet shoes.

The sight of a little wayside inn just ahead cheered me. I ducked under its overhanging thatched roof and collapsed on a crude, wooden bench. Before I had a chance to say anything, the innkeeper gave me a huge mug of hot, sweet tea. I put my coins on the table, but he waved them aside.

The men in the shop had stopped talking when I came in, but when they resumed their conversation it was about my colleague and me and the work we were doing in their village. Then one turned to me and began questioning. Why was I out on such a dismal day? Where was I going?

I told them my story. They clicked their tongues in sympathy. I had done well to come so far, they said. The road ahead was not steep. I had been over the worst part. I would be able to make it. A little farther up the way I might even find someone with a Landrover or a Jeep who would give me a ride. Thus they encouraged and supported me.

Not a little cheered and strengthened, I rose to go. Then one of the men came over and picked up my little suitcase.

"I will go with you the rest of the way and carry your case," he said quietly. "You are tired and ill, and I will help you."

"But if you carry my case," I protested, "what can I do for you?"

He smiled. "You already have done something for me. You care for my people." He smiled again. "Come, let us go. Together we shall make it."

As we stepped into the rain I forgot my weakness and drew strength from my unschooled mountain brother who walked beside me. I knew that together we would make it.

This is the picture behind Paul's words to the Galatians: "Bear one another's burdens, and so fulfil the law of Christ" (Gal. 6:2).

The Greek word used for "burden" is *baros* (BAH-russ), referring to something heavy or burdensome, a physical weight or a burden which has to be carried. *Baros* also may be a psychological need that makes us heavyhearted or a financial need that weighs heavily on our minds. In short, *baros* is anything that places a heavy demand on our inadequate resources.

Baros is also the word used to describe the weight sin imposes on us. And Paul writes of our need to bear with others when they slip into sin. J. B. Phillips has paraphrased Paul's words in this way: "Even if a man should be detected in some sin, my brothers, the spiritual ones among you should quietly set him back on the right path, not with any feeling of superiority but being yourselves on guard against temptation. Carry each other's burdens and so live out the law of Christ" (Gal. 6:1-2).

That is, if my brothers or sisters slip and fall into sin, instead of sitting, wagging my finger, clicking my tongue, and saying, "I knew you'd do it again!" in love and gentleness we assure them of Christ's forgiveness and pick them up and hold their hand. Then together we shall continue on our way, and together we shall make it.

One burden, however, we must bear alone: the burden of our personal accountability to God. Paul writes: "Let every man learn to assess properly the value of his own work and he can then be glad when he has done something worth doing without depending on the approval of others. For every man must 'shoulder his own pack'" (Gal. 6:4-5 Phillips). "For each man will have to bear his own load" (RSV).

The Greek word used here for load or burden is *phortion* (for-TEE-on). *Phortion* does not carry the connotation of weight, but rather simply something that has to be borne.

As an individual I, and I alone, am accountable to God for the way in which I obey his call, spend my time, and use or misuse the talents, abilities, and resources with which he has entrusted me. This is my own private "pack" which I, as a Christian soldier, must carry.

But this "burden" need not rest heavily on me. Christ has invited me to share it with him. "Take my yoke upon you, and learn from me; for I am gentle and lowly in heart," he says. "My yoke is easy [that is, fits well], and my burden is light" (Matt. 11:29-30).

The secret lies in turning our wills over to God. When our hearts have been captured by his love, it will not be a burden but a joy to obey him. Obeying him will, however, lead to bearing burdens for others. Though others' burdens sometimes may seem heavy, bearing them brings immense rewards and joy.

Alone we shall give account for our lives to God. But together you and I, and all who confess Jesus as Lord, travel through life, bearing one another's burdens. And together we shall make it.

Let us pray.

Teach us, good Lord, to serve Thee as Thou deservest; to give and not to count the cost; to fight and not to heed the wounds; to toil and not to seek for rest; to labor and not to ask for any reward save that of knowing that we do Thy will, through Jesus Christ, our Lord. Amen.   —Ignatius Loyola

Receive God's blessing.

May God "make all grace abound to you, so that in all things at all times, having all that you need, you will abound in every good work" (2 Cor. 9:8 NIV).

THE FIRST HANDFUL

Let us pray.

D̲ear Father, there is no way we can return to you as much as we have received. Your blessings and grace and love are far in excess of anything we could ever hope to offer. We can only humbly and gratefully receive from your hand, and seek to praise you. But we pray you will enable us to spill out generously to those with whom we come in contact. Help us to focus every day, not on receiving, but on giving. Make us both conscious and unconscious givers until at last giving will become the natural response of our heart. In Christ's name. Amen.

Our Bible reading is from Acts 20:24 and Colossians 3:17.

The meditation

I squatted on a stool in the low-ceilinged kitchen of my older Nepali friend, "Auntie" Ruth, and watched as she began to prepare the evening meal. The kitchen was simple—hard-packed mud floor, whitewashed mud walls, two small wood-shuttered windows without glass. In the corner was the foot-and-a-half high mud stove with holes on the top

138

over which to set kettles, and two holes on the side through which to push sticks of wood or shovel in charcoal. Black-bottomed pots and pans and large wooden spoons and ladles hung from hooks in the ceiling. Tin containers of various sizes and shapes, sitting on the floor, stored rice, sugar, tea, flour, salt, and water. Against one wall stood a couple of shelves screened over with a printed cloth curtain, behind which were stored a few cheap glasses and brass plates, bowls, and goblets.

Auntie Ruth was humming a happy little tune as she opened a large tin and began to scoop out handfuls of rice. But the first handful went, not into the large cooking pot, but into another tin. Puzzled, I asked, "Why did you put the first handful in that other tin, Auntie?"

Auntie Ruth was washing the rice, swishing it back and forth.

"Oh, that," she said matter-of-factly. "That is my thank offering. The Lord always gets the first handful. After the tin is filled, I either bring it to the church to be given to the hungry poor or I weigh it, determine its worth, and then bring the cash to church as my thank offering." She looked across at me and smiled. "I suppose you could say it is one of the ways we say 'table grace.'"

The Greeks of Paul's day followed a somewhat similar custom. At the beginning of each meal they would fill a small cup with wine and pour it out on the ground as a thank offering, a type of "table grace." *Spendesthai* (SPEN-des-thigh) is the Greek word meaning "a libation poured out as an offering to their god." Paul picks up this figure of speech in writing to the Philippian Christians when he says, "Even if I am to be poured as a libation upon the sacrificial offering of your faith, I am glad and rejoice with you all. Likewise you also should be glad and rejoice with me" (Phil. 2:17-18).

At the time Paul was imprisoned. He knew not what hour a guard would summon him to his death. As he wrote to his friends, Paul envisioned his blood, like red wine, being spilled out on the ground. "My blood," he is saying, "will be like a thank offering to God for the gift of life that enabled me to help you know God. If I can offer this kind of a thank offering to God, I shall rejoice, and I want you to rejoice with me."

Few of us will be called upon to spill out our blood in sacrifice for our faith or the faith of others. But I think, even as Paul saw a symbolic meaning in the libation, so we can see for ourselves a symbolic meaning. The libation was an offering poured on the ground. The wine quickly mingled with the clay and was forgotten and trodden underfoot. Once it was offered, no one paid any more attention to it.

This type of offering symbolizes a way of life that contrasts sharply with today's narcissism or self-centeredness. It symbolizes the selfless service many in our congregations pour out year after year. They arrive early at church Sunday mornings to unlock doors and cook coffee. They scrub coffee urns and clean kitchens, weed and mow church lawns, repair broken doors, paint, scrub, and varnish. They keep records and send out church mailings. They do all the routine housekeeping chores required to keep a congregation functioning smoothly. Their service is a type of table grace, the first "handful" of their time offered to God in thanksgiving for the gift of life and strength that God has given them. Because they look upon their work in this way, they willingly and cheerfully carry on, seeking no public recognition or praise. Their unselfish service says to the other members of the congregation: "If some of my hours can be spent to make it possible for you to know God and grow in his grace, then I rejoice and am glad. And I want you to rejoice with me. I consider my chores no hardship, but rather my way of saying thank you to God."

And we, in turn, who week after week receive the benefits of their loving service, would say thank you to God by offering to him the use of whatever talents and gifts he has given us. The contents of the handfuls we offer him will vary from person to person, but we all have something to give—and it is important that our offerings be the first handful. For Paul, it was not only the first handful, either, but his entire life. If we truly love our Lord, this will be our attitude also as we seek concrete ways of saying thank you to him. And our handfuls will complement one another, each gift making a contribution to the common good.

Let us pray.

Lord, teach us that work is giving hands and feet to love. Teach us to clean rooms as if you, our beloved Savior, were to occupy those rooms, to tend the grounds even as if you were to walk through them. Help us to infuse all work we do with a part of ourselves, and to know that you stand by watching, pleased and satisfied. Amen.

Receive God's blessing.

May the Giver of all good and perfect gifts enable you to make your lives a gift of love to those around you. May our gracious God strengthen and empower you to give with thanks, that your whole life might be one of joyful and continual thanksgiving. Amen.

141

WHAT REALLY COUNTS?

Let us pray.

Our minds are in many different places, Lord, filled with many different thoughts. Bring our minds and our hearts into focus on you. Amen.

Our Bible reading is from Philippians 1:8 and 27.

The meditation

My brother Paul slipped his pack onto the floor and leaned back in his chair, a look of satisfaction on his face. My eyes caught sight of the crown of everlasting flowers circling the brim of his hat.

"You made it to the top of Kilimanjaro!" I exclaimed.

He nodded.

All of us who lived on Mount Kilimanjaro, Africa's highest mountain, knew the Africans presented that crown of flowers only to those who were successful in scaling Kibo's summit. Broad-bosomed Kilimanjaro does not repel climbers with crags, cliffs, or ice falls, but its altitude, 19,342 feet, does prevent many from reaching the top. Crowns of everlasting flowers are not easily won.

142

The Greeks in the apostle Paul's day also observed the practice of rewarding winning athletes with crowns. Their crowns were intertwined with wild olive leaves, green parsley, and aromatic bay leaves. Greek contestants vied for those leafy crowns as avidly as athletes today compete for gold Olympic medals. When an athlete won a crown, he wore it proudly.

Paul referred to the athlete's crown when he called the Philippian Christians "my joy and crown" (Phil. 4:1 KJV). The Greek word for "crown" used here is *stephanos* (STEF-ah-nos), athlete's crown.

Stephanos, the leafy crown, had a second usage also. It was the crown presented to guests when they sat at a feast.

In India, when I was the honored guest in a home, I often would be greeted by a daughter of the family placing a floral lei around my neck. The people of Hawaii still follow this custom, as every tourist knows. On the mainland it is more customary to give a corsage or boutonniere.

The Greeks placed the leafy *stephanos* crowns on the heads of their guests to welcome and honor them. So in calling the Philippians his crown, Paul was saying: "You are the priceless prize with which I shall be crowned after running the race. You are my reward for all the hours of discipline and training, for the pain I endured when I entered into your hurt with you, for the narrowed, restricted life I have had to live. You also are the crown I shall wear when I sit down at the marriage feast of the Lamb, for you are my joy."

Paul's deepest satisfaction was in seeing what the grace of God was able to do in the hearts and lives of people. People were his chief concern. It was people who counted, not programs, not flamboyant

143

shows, not big meetings, not accolades for being the outstanding preacher of the year or the most successful church developer. No, what counted was what happened in the hearts and lives of people— a business woman like Lydia, a law-and-order man like the jailer, a slave like Onesimus. Immoral people, self-centered people, people struggling with sinful natures. Common, ordinary people, whose hearts and lives had been touched and changed by the Lord—these brought Paul his deepest joy. "You are my joy and my crown," he declared.

So too it was for Sir Henry Holland, the little puckish missionary surgeon of the Northwest Frontier of Pakistan. Leading ophthalmologists from all over the world came to observe Sir Holland perform surgeries. But skilled professional that he was, Sir Holland never lost the human touch. In *Adventures for God,* Clarence Hall recounts this incident.

> One day an old couple, both completely blinded by double cataracts, stumbled into his compound. They had not seen each other for years. Holland operated, then placed them in beds side by side in the hospital ward. Days later, when the bandages were removed simultaneously, they looked at each other with first, unbelief, then sheer enchantment. As the two old people went into each other's arms, tears of joy flowing down their faces, Holland wept with them.

Nor was Sir Holland's concern for the souls of people ever submerged by a heavy work load. Before each operation he would pray. He wanted, he declared, every healing event to be "a testimony to the tender mercy of God." When some colleagues objected to his mixing evangelism with his medical work, Sir Holland snapped: "I am a *missionary* doctor. The Christian medical man who says everything about the body and nothing about the soul is not doing his full duty."

How is it with us? Do we sometimes lose sight of the unprecedented value of people? Are needs of the heart pushed to the background in our big drives to build huge church buildings, pay off mortgages, or develop extensive programs? Do committee meetings take preference to home calls? Are we more concerned about people's physical and intellectual needs than about their spiritual needs?

Or, conversely, are we so absorbed in only preaching and teaching that we forget hungry people rarely can hear? Does running an organization make us so busy that people hesitate to call us when they are troubled? Wherein do we find our joy and our deepest satisfaction? Can we say about those we have been enabled to help come to know God, "You are my joy and my crown"? Or have we been so busy in other church work that we don't have a crown like that to wear yet?

Let us pray.

Slow us down, Lord. Caught in a whirlwind of things to be done, places to go, and people to see, our vision often blurs, and in seeing much, we do not really see at all. Steady us. Help us take time to see, to reach out, to touch those who, through us, experience you.

Receive God's blessing.

May the Lord make you increase and abound in love to one another and to all people, so he may establish your hearts unblamable in holiness before our God and Father, at the coming of our Lord Jesus with all his saints. Amen.

WALKING INTO THE WIND

Let us pray.

Speak words of courage to our hearts, O Jesus, that we may endure triumphantly. Amen.

Our Bible reading is from 2 Corinthians 4:8-10, 16-18.

The meditation

Zoe, a vibrant 13-year-old, can hobble around only on crutches. Her twisted body attracts stares that for years caused her to withdraw inside herself. Then Zoe met the Lord Jesus. A new hope sprang to birth in her heart. She gave it expression one day when she impulsively asked a friend, "When we get to heaven will you run around with me?"

The hope Zoe cherishes that things will be better for her in the future enables her to be steadfast in her trials and to face life with a positive, thankful attitude. Her face radiates joy.

Zoe is not alone. Many people with varying afflictions make up this community of suffering ones who need a unique type of patience and steadfastness.

The Greek word for this particular kind of patience or endurance is *hupomone* (hu-po-moe-NAY).

146

Let us consider the different literary works in which the word is found, and its meaning.

We find *hupomone* first in classical Greek, where the word meant the "grin-and-bear-it" stoicism we are forced into when calamities over which we have no control descend on us.

Hupomone was used also to describe the toughness of plants that survive adverse situations. The mesquite bush, for example, sends its tap root probing underground, 40, 50 feet down until it reaches water. Thus it is able to survive the shimmering heat of the desert.

Hupomone is also used in the Second Book of Maccabees, one of the apocryphal books, where it describes the spiritual staying power enabling people to die for their God.

In the New Testament, the word becomes even richer in meaning. The noun appears 30 times, and the corresponding verb about 15 times. It describes a patience or steadfastness growing only in the soil of affliction and trial. In Revelation John says: "I John, your brother . . . share with you in Jesus the tribulation and the kingdom and the patient endurance" (Rev. 1:9).

Three other words often are linked with *hupomone:* faith, hope, and joy. We readily can understand why, for *hupomone* is the patience that comes from believing things will be better in the future. The persecuted Christians could hope for relief only after death. However, *hupomone* is used also to describe enduring suffering in the hope that one's loved ones will come to know Christ in this life.

Faith that things will be better can be so vibrant that it brings hope also to the immediate present and transforms daily living. *Hupomone* enables us to declare about testings, "These will lead to glory."

147

Hupomone is not the stoic endurance of waiting for night when sleep will blot out the hurt. It is the plucky stalwartness that can greet the dawn of a new day with a kiss, welcoming another opportunity to prove the faithfulness of God. Faith begets hope, and hope lights the lamp of joy within.

James holds up Job as an example of this patience or fortitude. The story of Job pictures realistically and vividly the fight involved in learning to endure in this way. One does not glide easily into this steadfastness. *Hupomone* is hewn out in the midst of storms.

You remember Job's story. Marauding bandits plundered his caravans. Cattle hustlers whisked away his herds and murdered his farm workers. A tornado flattened his house and buried alive his children. Then Job broke out with sores. To add to his misery, his friends said he was to blame for it all, and in fact, he really wasn't getting all he deserved!

Job reacted, first in shock and pious resignation. But then, as the reality of his losses got through to him, he alternately plunged into despair, lashed out in anger, stoutly insisted he was innocent, asked "Why?" and evidenced jealousy of those not afflicted as he was. Up and down an emotional roller coaster Job flew. Through it all, however, he never questioned the existence of God. Nor did he ever voice the desire to walk out on God, mad at him though he was.

Job lived before Christ's death and resurrection ushered in a new age of faith and hope and joy for believers. But even Job caught faint fleeting glimpses of a Mediator who would plead his case. And finally a personal encounter with God brought deep inner peace, the serenity born of the faith that

God is in control and that he will work out everything for the best in the end. This faith gives birth to *hupomone,* the patience that can endure, even joyfully, situations that cannot be changed.

George Matheson was deserted by the woman he loved after he lost his sight. He prayed he would be able to accept this "not with dumb resignation, but with holy joy; not only with the absence of murmur, but with a song of praise."

Hupomone, then, is not walking with one's back to the wind, but turning and facing it, walking into it and exulting in pitting one's endurance against its strength.

Hupomone is Stephen, not crumpled on the ground, cringing as he awaits, trembling, the blows of the rocks that will pound life out of him. *Hupomone* rather is Stephen, standing erect, his shining face lifted heavenward.

Finally, *hupomone* is singing with old Luther:

> Take they then, what they will:
> Life, goods, yea all, and still
> The kingdom ours remaineth!

Let us pray.

> When we seek relief
> From a long-felt grief,
> When temptations come alluring
> Make us patient and enduring;
> Show us that bright shore
> Where we weep no more.
>
> Jesus, still lead on,
> Till our rest be won;
> Heavenly leader, still direct us,
> Still support, console, protect us,
> Till we safely stand
> In our Father's land. Amen.

> —Nicolaus Ludwig von Zinzendorf

Receive God's blessing.

As you pass through deep waters, may the God who created you be with you. When troubles come, may they not overwhelm you. When you pass through life, may you not be burned, and may the hard trials that come not destroy you. For God, your Savior, loves you. He will be with you, and he will save you. Amen.

paraboleuomai
(pa-ra-boh-LOO-oh-my)
to gamble; to risk

GAMBLERS

Let us pray.

O God, help us to find the wisdom to know what is right, and the faith and courage to do it. Give us a fresh glimpse of your power and love. We pray in the mighty name of Jesus. Amen.

Our Bible reading is from Matthew 8:18-22.

The meditation

What counsel would you have given in the following situation? One day at our Bible college in East Africa, Frederick, one of our students who had renounced his Moslem faith to be baptized as a Christian, had just received letters from his parents. His father wrote: "If you come home, I'll kill you." His mother wrote: "If you don't come home, I'll hang myself."

"What shall I do?" Frederick asked.

We prayed. Finally Frederick decided he would risk going home. The result was that after a few months his parents also were baptized.

For Frederick things turned out happily. Others pay a price.

The Greek word for "risk" is *paraboleuomai* (pa-ra-boh-LOO-oh-my). Associated with gambling, it implies willingness to take a risk, not knowing

151

whether those who play the game will win or lose. It all depends on how the dice roll.

A group of the first Christians coined the name *parabolani* (pa-ra-boh-LAH-nee), from *paraboleuomai*, for those willing to gamble personal safety by visiting prisons and nursing people ill with contagious or terminal illnesses. In the decades that followed, this spirit of unconcern for self continued. In A.D. 252, plague broke out in Carthage. People fled in terror, leaving the dead and dying in their beds. Cyprian, the Christian bishop, summoned his people. They organized into teams, moved into the city, buried the dead, and nursed the sick and dying. Risking their own lives, they saved the city from total destruction.

The late 1800s and early 1900s saw a sweeping missionary movement as people risked death at the hands of suspicious peoples or tropical diseases. Among them was Father Heyer, who thought that his chances of dying early in India were so great that he had a coffin built so it would be ready when he died. But Father Heyer lived more than 80 years and saw a large Christian congregation come into being.

Even in our comfort-accustomed age, a few brave people are willing to take risks. I think of the mother in Los Angeles who felt her daughter shaking her awake one night.

"Mom," the girl said, "these three young fellows stopped in at our meeting at church tonight. They've no place to stay. I've brought them home. Can they stay with us?"

The mother got up, fed the boys, made up beds, laundered their clothes, and cared for them for a number of days. As a result, one of the boys wended his way back to his parents in the Midwest.

In all of these cases, the dice rolled right. But sometimes those who run the risk suffer loss.

A missionary couple spent their early retirement years in Africa. Among other activities, they visited prisons. Once in the dead of night they awakened to see a naked man towering over their bed, knife in hand, his dark body glistening from the oil he had rubbed on so he could not be grabbed and caught. We suspected this unwelcome visitor had heard the elderly couple preach in prison but had not opened his heart to the gospel.

Many others took risks for their faith—and lost.

The cruel gossip of "respectable" fellow church members ripped to shreds the reputation of a man trying to reach prostitutes for Christ.

A young woman who refused to go to bed with company executives lost her job.

A mother who instructed her children in the Christian faith toiled for seven years in a labor camp in Russia.

A businessman, asked to be dishonest in his transactions, forfeited his pension and had to retrain for other work.

A congregation in a changing community lost members when the pastor and church council introduced a program to include the new "foreign-speaking" residents of the community.

A few, even in our age, have lost all, from a human point of view, as they have laid down their lives as martyrs.

Taking risks for Christ, when he calls us to do so, is worthy of honor and recognition, the apostle Paul declared. Epaphroditus, a Christian from Philippi, risked identification with Paul by coming to be with him in prison. In writing about Epaphroditus to the Philippian congregation, as Epaphroditus antici-

153

pated returning to them, Paul wrote: "Welcome him in the Lord with great joy! You should hold men like him in highest honor, for his loyalty to Christ brought him very near death—he risked his life to do for me in person what distance prevented you all from doing" (Phil. 2:29-30 Phillips).

To be a member of the *parabolani*—those who take risks, not knowing for certain what the outcome will be—calls for both conviction and courage. But the church and a decent society cannot continue to exist without such people.

Sir Henry Holland, whose skilled surgery brought sight to 100,000 of the blind in the robber-infested Northwest Frontier of Pakistan, prayed every night he would scorn the way of safety so God's will might be done. At 82 he upbraided an assembly of youth in London for their lack of spirit. "The grave is secure," he said, "but terribly dull. Serve your age well and security will take care of itself."

Parabolani. The gamblers who, willing to risk all, are prepared to accept loss and failure as well as gain and success, because they believe in what they are doing.

What risks are you willing to take?

Let us pray.

Courage is what we need, O Lord, courage and conviction, and love and loyalty to you and a fresh vision of your saving power. Embolden us, O Lord, that we may be true *parabolani*. In Christ's name. Amen.

Receive God's blessing.

May God strengthen you so you will be able to hold up your limp arms and steady your trembling knees as you commit yourself to him. Amen.

WHAT! NOT SELF-ASSERTIVE?

Let us pray.

O Jesus, Suffering Servant of God, sometimes it is hard to follow you because you lead us over paths that seem strange to us, paths where we have to die a little more to ourselves. Give us courage to continue with you, Jesus, and show us which path to take. Amen.

Our Bible reading is Mark 15:21.

The meditation

Her skinny arms and legs dangled loosely from her 13-year-old, flat-chested body. Her braided hair was the color of wheat stalks gathered in a sheaf. Her huge eyes were blue and full of fear. Those eyes, looking so intently at people, asked why so much was demanded of her — asked but received no answer.

The people of Belgium had not desired war. World War II had boomed and blasted around them until finally it overflowed the borders and swept into their little, defenseless land too. Every morning now alien men in uniforms ordered her into a

155

truck and hauled her to a bombed-out city where she toiled all day, shoveling refuse and debris into wheelbarrows. Her back ached ceaselessly. The palms of her hands ran with blood. Blood was in her throat too. When she swallowed, she often tasted it.

What was hardest of all to bear was that the pride had gone out of the eyes of her people. The aliens were grinding them underfoot. The humiliation of having to submit was more bitter than horseradish. But they had no choice, for when a small country is occupied by an enemy force, the residents become but puppets, pulled this way and that on the strings of the ruling army. They are *compelled* to serve.

Aggareuo (ahng-gah-ROO-oh) was the Greek word for this state of being compelled to serve whether or not one liked it. The nations that had bowed under Greek, Roman, Persian, or Syrian rule knew well its meaning.

The word came first from the Persians. *Aggaros* (AHNG-gah-ross) was the base word. It meant "courier." The Persians utilized men and horses in occupied countries to set up the most efficient postal or courier system the world had known. They tested horses to see how far they could run at top speed. At the exhaustion point they erected a small post and assigned an official there to have a fresh horse and rider ready when the first lathered, panting horse heaved to a stop. The courier routes crisscrossed the country. Night and day horses ran whipped and lashed by their riders, and thus the official messages were carried from city to city. No man in any occupied village knew when he or his horses might be compelled to run the route.

Invading armies also pressed the inhabitants of

156

the land into carrying packs for officers or wounded soldiers. Property was not exempt either. Boats, houses, animals — all were at the mercy of the invading aliens.

"Do not resist or murmur," the people were warned. "If you do, you will be beaten and lose all you have."

It was also because this custom was so prevalent in the land that Simon of Cyrene was one day compelled to bear the heavy cross of the Lord Jesus. The fact that it was the cross of a "criminal" made it even more humiliating.

What does all this mean to us? No enemy army has ever overrun our country.

In the Sermon on the Mount, Jesus said: "If any one forces you to go one mile, go with him two miles." The Living Bible retains the military picture: "If the military demand that you carry their gear for a mile, carry it two" (Matt. 5:41).

Jesus is saying: "If someone compels you to do something you feel he hasn't a right to ask you to do, if someone orders you around and doesn't respect your wishes, if you have to do something you really don't want to do, do it. And do it with good will, for this is my way."

I think of one instance when I felt myself forced into a responsibility I didn't want. At the time of resettlement of the Vietnamese refugees, our church council met to consider sponsoring a family. I asked some questions. Did they realize what was involved in giving the needed emotional and moral support to displaced orphaned people? Who would do it? Would people be willing to continue giving this support month after month, year after year, as long as it was needed? My parental family had sponsored a displaced Estonian couple and their children after World War II, and I knew a little about what was involved, I said. Though I wouldn't put it into words, I knew part of my reluctance came because I was tired of bearing the burdens of others. I had been heavily involved in a number of hurting situations, and I didn't want to have to enter into the pain of another so soon. When the congregation voted to sponsor a family, I abstained, but silently I told the Lord I wanted him to know that somebody else would be assuming this responsibility. And I made this clear to others too.

An attractive, brilliant, young woman with four small children, whose husband had not been able to escape from Vietnam, was assigned to our congregation. In company with her was a cousin, a beautiful girl in her early 20s.

Shortly after our congregation had received them, one of the members of the committee called me. The committee felt it would be good for the family to attend a week at a family Bible camp, she said. They understood I would be at the camp, and they were asking me to be sponsor for the family for the week.

I felt resentment rising within. I had wanted that week for my own private rest and renewal. Did they really think the family would enjoy a week at a camp where people were strangers? I argued. But the committee stood firm, and I felt I had no choice. I felt as though I was being pressed into service.

Mercifully God dealt with my stubborn, selfish heart, so that when in the course of the week all the hurt and pain and shock of the last months in Saigon were poured out, I was able to respond fully. And out of the relationship that was born that week grew a deep friendship and love that has enhanced and enriched my life as few friendships have done before.

I was pressed into service. I accepted grudgingly. But God brought blessing out of it. How aptly my experience reflects Michel Quoist's observation:

> Don't worry, God says, you have gained all,
> While men came in to you
> I, your God
> Slipped in among them.

"If any one forces you to go one mile, go with him two miles," Jesus says.

In a day of inordinate emphasis on individual fulfillment and self-development, with seminars and lectures to teach self-assertiveness and lives becoming more and more narcissistic, Jesus' words sound strange to our ears, but they are words to ponder.

Let us pray.

O Divine Master, grant that we may not so much seek to be consoled, as to console; to be understood, as to understand; to be loved, as to love; for it is in giving that we receive, it is in pardoning that we are pardoned, and it is in dying that we are born to Eternal Life. Amen. —St. Francis of Assisi

Receive God's blessing.

The Lord give you peace at all times, in all ways. Amen.